China, Nuclear Weapons, and Arms Control

A Preliminary Assessment

Chairmen's Report of a roundtable jointly sponsored by
the Council on Foreign Relations,
the National Defense University, and
the Institute for Defense Analyses

Robert A. Manning, Ronald Montaperto, Brad Roberts
Cochairs

The Council on Foreign Relations, Inc., a nonprofit, nonpartisan national organization founded in 1921, is dedicated to promoting understanding of international affairs through the free and civil exchange of ideas. The Council's members are dedicated to the belief that America's peace and prosperity are firmly linked to that of the world. From this flows the mission of the Council: to foster America's understanding of other nations—their peoples, cultures, histories, hopes, quarrels, and ambitions—and thus to serve our nation through study and debate, private and public.

THE COUNCIL TAKES NO INSTITUTIONAL POSITION ON POLICY ISSUES AND HAS NO AFFILIATION WITH THE U.S. GOVERNMENT. ALL STATEMENTS OF FACT AND EXPRESSIONS OF OPINION CONTAINED IN ALL ITS PUBLICATIONS ARE THE SOLE RESPONSIBILITY OF THE AUTHOR OR AUTHORS.

From time to time books, monographs, reports, and papers written by members of the Council's research staff or others are published as a "Council on Foreign Relations Publication." Any work bearing that designation is, in the judgment of the Committee on Studies of the Council's Board of Directors, a responsible treatment of a significant international topic.

For further information about this Council paper, please write the Council on Foreign Relations, 58 East 68th Street, New York, NY 10021, or call the Director of Communications at (212) 434-9400. Visit our website at *www.cfr.org*.

CONTENTS

FOREWORD

Few challenges loom as large on the U.S. foreign policy agenda as the effective management of relations with the People's Republic of China (PRC). This is a perennial challenge, given China's central role in Asia and the many issues on the bilateral agenda that feature prominently in U.S. domestic politics. But U.S.-PRC relations take on added significance with China's emergence after decades of isolation and its growing weight in the global economy. Cooperation between China and the United States could pay large dividends for the international system more generally—just as confrontation between them would have far-reaching implications.

The U.S.-PRC bilateral agenda is loaded with many contentious issues, including trade relations, human rights, regional security, and nonproliferation. During the last year or two, another issue has emerged: the strategic military dimension of the relationship, particularly the nuclear component. The Cox Committee report of spring 1999 was a dramatic wake-up call for many, sounding an alarm about China's emergence as a nuclear competitor of the United States and Beijing's apparent willingness to use all means to gain advantages. Beijing has sounded its own alarm—over the prospective U.S. deployment of both theater and national missile defenses. A new set of political-military issues is thus joining the traditional and already overloaded bilateral agenda.

The coming national election promises to put some of these issues at center stage. The debate over national missile defense is certain to focus in part on the impact that such defenses might have on China's strategic modernization program and the Chinese assertion that national missile defense is the impetus for that program. The next administration will have to buttress its electoral promises with a sound understanding of

U.S. interests vis-à-vis China's strategic modernization program and how best to secure outcomes consistent with U.S. interests and preferences.

Yet the new political-military issues on the U.S.-PRC agenda are as yet unfamiliar to most of those concerned with either the bilateral political relationship or strategic nuclear affairs. The Washington community that follows China policy has had little experience with the strategic and nuclear aspects of the relationship. The community that follows nuclear policy has had similarly little experience in thinking through China's emergence as a nuclear actor, given its focus on the U.S.-Russian relationship.

In order to bridge this gap, the Council on Foreign Relations helped form a roundtable in 1998. It found willing cosponsors in the National Defense University and the Institute for Defense Analyses. Under the cochairmanship of Robert A. Manning, Ronald Montaperto, and Brad Roberts, the group met initially in 1998 and then more regularly in 1999. The latter period saw the release of the Cox Committee report, NATO's accidental bombing of China's embassy in Belgrade, the test launch of a new generation of Chinese intercontinental ballistic missile, and intensifying concern over the PRC's relations with Taiwan.

This report summarizes the insights and lessons learned during the last two years. It should be read as a report of its coauthors and not of the roundtable membership more generally; indeed, members of the roundtable have not been asked to endorse its content. It is intended as a preliminary assessment, not as the last word. In fact, this report raises more questions than it answers. The ideas presented here are intended to provoke new discussion about China's role in shaping the nuclear future and how to best engage China on matters nuclear.

The report concludes that Beijing's policy choices vis-à-vis its strategic modernization program are likely to make it the nuclear actor whose behavior may matter most to Washington during the coming decade, and certainly more than has been appreciated. The tendency in Washington to dismiss China as an inconsequential nuclear actor must be set aside in favor of a clearer appreciation of China's significance, both current and potential. Over the coming decade China could very substantially increase the size, sophistication, and overall capability of its strategic force. It could do so in ways that jeopardize continued reductions by Russia in the Strategic Arms Reduction Talks process. It could respond to the deployment of theater missile defenses by proliferating countermeasure technologies to friendly client states. It could also make common cause with Russia to mount more aggressive opposition to U.S. engagement in surrounding regions. Or it could do none of these things. It could modernize its forces in a modest way, come to accept missile defenses as not only necessary but stabilizing, and continue to accept some form of partnership with the United States in promoting global institutions.

Of course, it is not up to Washington to decide how Beijing will proceed. China's trajectory may already be firmly decided, and the influence Washington might bring to bear both too little and too late. But this report proceeds from the assumption, well defended in the accompanying analysis, that it is possible for Washington to influence China's trajectory. If it is to have any hope of doing so, Washington needs a clearer understanding of the factors at play, the perceptions driving policy in Beijing, and the types of Chinese interests that might be engaged to achieve the necessary measure of cooperation.

The report begins with a detailed review of what is available in the public literature about the state of China's nuclear weapons capabilities and its strategic modernization program. The authors paint a picture that is in many ways disconcerting. Significant gaps in information exist, not least because of Beijing's own lack of transparency. Accordingly, misperceptions about China's capabilities seem very likely to have crept into the public debate. But it is clear that China is involved in a major modernization program, one that has been underway for more than a decade and that promises to continue for at least a decade into the future. The report then elaborates the forks that lie in the road toward strategic modernization. It considers also the impact of the modernization program on U.S. interests in regional security, nuclear safety, and international stability more generally.

Working from the premise that the United States has an interest in influencing China's choices as it approaches those forks, the report then turns to a discussion of how to approach China. The goal would be to gain a political understanding that China will not move toward the most destabilizing force structures in the years ahead. China's increasing participation in arms control regimes over the last decade is evaluated for what it suggests about China's future willingness to embrace new forms of restraint.

The report also flags the emerging triangular relationship between the United States, Russia, and China, as each reacts to developments in the strategic postures of the other two. These interrelationships are little explored in the United States today. Few U.S. analysts have any notion of the dynamic in the Sino-Russian leg of the triangle. The authors' call for further study of the offense/defense interrelationships among the three deserves broader consideration within the U.S. policy community.

The authors then recommend steps toward a strategy for testing Chinese intentions in this area and for beginning a strategic dialogue about the requirements of stability between the United States and China. The report does not explore the policy implications for the United States if Beijing and Washington fail to find a political agreement in the near future about the impact of China's strategic modernization and of U.S. ballistic missile defenses on each other's interests and plans. It does not set out to resolve the deep debate in the U.S. strategic community about whether stability requires that China possess a secure retaliatory force. These questions require answers of their own, and it is hoped that the information and analysis included here will be constructive toward that end.

Lawrence J. Korb
Maurice R. Greenberg Chair, Director of Studies
Council on Foreign Relations

ACKNOWLEDGMENTS

The three cochairs are grateful to their fellow members in the roundtable process for their curiosity about the larger picture and for the consistently thoughtful and creative dialogue during the course of our meetings. The two other cochairs wish to particularly acknowledge the leading role Brad Roberts played in summarizing the discussions and in preparing the initial draft of the report. We are also grateful to a number of individuals for providing off-the-record opening presentations in these meetings to help us get the discussion started, including Peter Almquist, Kurt Campbell, Wendy Frieman, Bates Gill, and Tom Woodrow.

We thank the many individuals who have given time and effort to comment constructively on the report as we have worked it through various drafts. From among members of the roundtable, we received especially detailed and useful critiques from Zachary Davis, Wendy Frieman, Bates Gill, James Mulvenon, David Shambaugh, and especially Jim Przystup. In addition, we benefited from reviews by some outside the study process, including Steve Cambone, Ralph Cossa, Alton Frye, and Victor Utgoff. As indicated elsewhere in this report, the roundtable also involved individuals from the Departments of State, Defense, and Energy, as well as the intelligence community, all participating in their private capacities. All were helpful in keeping us focused on real policy issues and on the changing substance of the policy agenda. Some of these individuals were also most helpful in working with the coauthors to ensure the highest possible degree of relevance and accuracy in the written report. We wish particularly to thank Peter Almquist and Dunbar Lockwood. We wish also to underscore that the coauthors alone have final responsibility for the accuracy of the information included here and for the structure and content of the argumentation.

We are grateful to the Council on Foreign Relations for publishing this report. We also want to express our gratitude to David Speedie and Patricia Nicholas of the Carnegie Corporation of New York, without whose timely and generous support this publication might not have been possible. This project was an ad hoc endeavor involving three cosponsoring institutions, not just the Council but also the Institute for Defense Analyses and the National Defense University. But we are very pleased that the Council has agreed to affiliate itself with this work and to make it available under the Council's auspices to a larger audience. Finally, we want to stress that the views in this report are solely those of the authors and do not represent the views of their respective organizations or any U.S. government agency.

Robert A. Manning
Ronald Montaperto
Brad Roberts

China, Nuclear Weapons, and Arms Control

Robert A. Manning, Ronald Montaperto, and Brad Roberts

EXECUTIVE SUMMARY

Historically, U.S. nuclear strategists and arms control experts have paid little attention to the People's Republic of China (PRC). China has not been a major factor in the U.S. nuclear calculus, which has remained centered on U.S.-Russian nuclear arsenals as the principal framework for arms control and arms reductions. Yet today China is the only one of the five de jure nuclear weapons states qualitatively and quantitatively expanding its nuclear arsenal.

In contrast to the Cold War nuclear paradigm that remains centered on Russia, this report offers the proposition that over the next decade or so, China's nuclear choices may matter to the United States at least as much as Russia's, if not more so. The report focuses on China's current nuclear deployments, the status of its nuclear modernization efforts, and its doctrinal debates, which offer hints at the trajectory and possible end-states of its nuclear modernization. The report also poses questions about the impact of China's nuclear program on U.S. and Russian arms control efforts and for the development of missile defenses.

This study is the product of a series of workshops focused on nuclear futures and U.S. security interests. In the course of our efforts, we found that:

- China's strategic force is postured differently from that of the United States. China has land-, air-, and sea-based nuclear capabilities, but its sea- and air-based components have little or no intercontinental capability. Beijing's ballistic missile force consists overwhelmingly of short- and intermediate-range missiles that are either dual-capable or armed with conventional warheads. It is constructed primarily to deal with China's security requirements around its periphery. China's strategic force is land-based and small, with only a few intercontinental ballistic missiles (ICBMs, currently estimated to number from six to twenty-four) capable of reaching targets in the continental United States.

- China is modernizing its strategic force. This process has been underway more or less continually over the past two decades and will continue for the foreseeable future regardless of U.S. behavior. Modernization has already brought a substantial increase in the number of missiles apparently targeted on U.S. allies in East Asia, in particular Taiwan and Japan. With its successful test of its DF-31 missile in summer 1999, Beijing is now moving to deploy a new generation of road-mobile, solid-fueled, long-range ICBMs capable of reaching targets across the western United States. The follow-on DF-41, scheduled for deployment late in this decade, is rumored to be capable of reaching targets anywhere in North America.

- For some time, Beijing has had the capability to deploy multiple warheads atop its current ICBM force—but it has chosen not to do so. Whether it can deploy or will deploy multiple warheads atop its DF-31 and DF-41 missiles in the absence of the constraints imposed by the Comprehensive Test Ban Treaty (CTBT) are hotly debated questions that cannot be answered on the basis of this unclassified assessment. But the potential for a substantial increase in the size and capability of China's long-range nuclear force clearly exists.

- Multiple factors account for China's modernization program. One is the reality that China's existing missile force is aging, and as Beijing fields new systems it would certainly want to make technological improvements. Another factor is a long-standing concern about the survivability of its deterrent force. With a small number of long-range delivery systems apparently deployed in readily targetable silos, China has been concerned for decades about its ability to absorb a first strike and to retaliate successfully. This concern has intensified over the last decade, as the United States has demonstrated a dramatic improvement in conventional, long-range, precision strike assets.

- The end of the Cold War refocused Chinese military planning from the Soviet Union to the United States. In thinking through conflict scenarios with the United States, Chinese planners focus on the threat of conflict over Taiwan. Beijing apparently believes that advanced missile capabilities can be leveraged to secure its goals with respect to Taiwan without actual invasion. It apparently sees short-range missiles as useful for political coercion, and, if necessary, for defeating Taiwanese military forces, while its long-range missiles induce restraint by the United States.

- China's modernization program has proceeded in parallel with a debate over nuclear doctrine. The strategy of minimum deterrence embodied in the existing small retaliatory force is subjected to growing criticism. The objective conditions that shaped China's nuclear strategy in the 1950s and 1960s are not the conditions shaping nuclear strategy debates today. As a result, there is a small but intense debate in Washington about China's current strategy—whether it has moved from minimum deterrence to limited deterrence, implying the need for a more substantial operational capability. There is also some evidence that Chinese nuclear strategy is becoming increasingly differentiated, with minimum deterrence continuing to govern the strategic level, while a counterforce strategy, driven largely by developments in South Asia, is evolving at the regional level.

- While China is increasing the size and capability of its strategic nuclear arsenal, the ultimate parameters of China's future strategic force are an open question. As developmental programs reach fruition, China will face multiple programmatic and resource questions related to the number of systems it deploys and their specific technical attributes.

- Rigorous analysis of China's strategic capabilities is hindered by the tight lid of military secrecy Beijing maintains over virtually all information regarding its nuclear program. The problem is not only a lack of transparency, however; concealment and deception appear to be integral to China's approach to the entire range of issues associated with its nuclear posture. In the absence of official and firm data, we were left to work with a hodgepodge of often contradictory information, usually leaked to or rumored in the media. The conclusions herein reflect our best judgment based on data available in the public domain.

What will determine the type of force China ultimately deploys?
A number of factors will shape the decision. The fate of China's economic reforms will certainly play a role. If reform accelerates, and if China becomes more prosperous and pluralistic, Beijing may be less likely to have an adversarial relationship with the United States and more prone to exercise restraint on the size and posture of its nuclear force.

However, we are not persuaded that economic factors will be paramount. Clearly, military modernization remains the lowest of the four modernization priorities, and, within the military domain, nuclear matters have not traditionally commanded the highest priority. But most of the industrial and technological infrastructure is already in place to allow Beijing to construct a larger force. These are sunk costs. Increased capability would bring new but incremental costs, not an order-of-magnitude increase in the demand for scarce resources. If Beijing finds that national security requires a larger investment in strategic forces, it is likely to find a way to pay for it.

Internationally, China's nuclear planning environment is growing increasingly complex. The emergence of an unexpected nuclear and missile dynamic in South Asia is unwelcome in Beijing, despite its years of assistance to Pakistan. Nuclear reemphasis and the prospect of nuclear chaos in Russia are alarming as well. Japan continues to be a major concern in China's view of the nuclear future. But the key international factor is the United States. Policymakers in Beijing are focused on the bilateral relationship with the United States and on how Beijing can use improving strategic capabilities to secure its interests vis-à-vis Washington.

Chinese policymakers are concerned with a number of worrisome factors in the evolving U.S.-PRC relationship. One is a perception, frequently stated publicly, of an assertive United States, motivated by hegemonic ambitions to contain and encircle China and to frustrate its emergence as a coequal great power. They see a United States moving to increase its ability to project military power by conventional military means, to exploit Russia's decline to lock in its strategic advantages with large stocks of nuclear weapons, and to field defenses in order to secure military supremacy in perpetuity. Some in China seem to believe that new nuclear strength would help to remedy their own sense of powerlessness in the face of U.S. preeminence.

The prospect of theater ballistic missile defense and/or national missile defense (NMD) deployments by the United States presents China with both an operational military challenge and a political threat. Most immediately, Beijing is concerned that such deployments will reinforce the drift toward independence by Taiwan. Chinese officials have harshly criticized missile defense systems as destabilizing.

Moreover, Chinese strategists view the prospect of NMD deployments by the United States as threatening to the survivability of China's own deterrent. Chinese spokesmen also articulate a concern that U.S. NMD deployments would be exploited by Washington to coerce decision-makers in Beijing to do Washington's bidding over Taiwan and anywhere else where interests or values might clash. Consequently, Chinese nuclear planners have begun to plan based on worst-case scenarios against the prospect of a viable, robust NMD system. In this sense, there is an interactive relationship between U.S. decisions on missile defense deployments and the end-state of China's nuclear modernization.

In our view, no one factor is likely to determine decisions in Beijing about the key operational parameters of China's future strategic force. Depending on which factors gain priority in thinking in Beijing, China is likely to debate five basic options for its future force:

- *To stay small but be modern.* In this scenario, China is motivated primarily to "stay in the game" and would bet on force mobility, as well as improved penetration aids and countermeasures, in its offensive forces to deal with the survivability challenge.

- *To restore minimum deterrence.* In this scenario, China is motivated primarily to pace the deployment of defenses by the United States with increases in its own forces in ways that give it confidence that twenty or so warheads will be capable of reaching U.S. targets.

- *To opt for regional dominance and interim global irrelevance.* In this scenario, China is motivated primarily by the desire to stay ahead of India and other proliferators in Asia and is unmotivated at this time to compete on a new basis with the United States and Russia.

- *To construct a force de frappe.* In this scenario, China is motivated to hedge its bets at both the regional and global levels by developing a force large and capable enough "to tear off an arm" of even the largest adversary.

- *To construct a parity force.* In this scenario, China is motivated to field a very robust force as part of a political strategy to signal its ascendance over Russia, its leading role in Asia, and its equal footing with America on the world scene.

In our judgment, China's debate is likely to focus on the middle three options. Given China's secrecy and lack of transparency on nuclear issues, this underscores the importance of testing China's will to continue with past restraint and the necessity of engaging Beijing in a meaningful, two-way strategic dialogue that serves to inform and illuminate Chinese thinking on these and related questions.

In thinking through China's options in this way, two important themes stand out. One is the clear emergence of a U.S.-Sino-Russian strategic triangle. China is concerned about possible Russian reactions to U.S. missile defenses, including the possibility of Russia's own deployment of improved defenses; the abandonment of nuclear reductions, and renunciation of the treaties on Intermediate-range Nuclear Forces (INF) and on Conventional Forces in Europe (CFE). Each contingency independently or together in some combination would have significant repercussions for Chinese military planners. Meanwhile Moscow is concerned about possible Chinese reactions to bilateral U.S.-Russian offensive reductions as well as U.S. defensive deployments. The prospect that China might seek to substantially increase its nuclear force is likely to diminish even further Russia's willingness in the strategic reductions process to relinquish a significant up-load capability. The latter includes both stored warheads and missile delivery systems that it can equip with multiple warheads.

The emerging triangular strategic offense/defense relationship among these three powers is intellectual terra incognita. The concepts and methodologies developed in the bipolar Cold War context appear ill-suited to understanding the dynamics of this new relationship.

The other important theme is the apparent failure to date in the U.S. debate over ballistic missile defenses (BMD) to adequately take into account the China factor. That debate has focused on how to construct a defense large and effective enough to deal with the so-called rogue states without also calling into question the viability of Russia's deterrent. Only in the second half of 1999 did we begin to hear analysts in Washington debate whether China should be treated as a "small Russia" or a "big rogue"—i.e., as a country whose deterrent the United States should seek to preserve or negate. In our view, most advocates of BMD have dismissed China's possible reactions to theater missile defense (TMD) and NMD as having little more than nuisance value, while most opponents of BMD have embraced those possible reactions as yet another reason to reject deployments.

In our view, it is time to assess realistically possible Chinese reactions to NMD and to consider whether it is possible to induce China to define its future forces in ways that best serve U.S. interests. This requires first and foremost a clear notion of U.S. interests.

One key interest is to maximize the benefits of whatever defenses that the United States chooses to deploy. At the outset, the possibility of a best-case response to U.S. diplomatic efforts cannot be dismissed: namely, China's acquiescence. However, the possibility of a worst-case response by Beijing cannot be dismissed either. Such a scenario could entail a large buildup of China's strategic forces; efforts to induce Russia to abandon further strategic reductions and perhaps even to redeploy certain assets; and the sharing of countermeasure technologies for effective defeat of defenses with the so-called rogues. In other words, by deploying defenses without an eye to possible Chinese reactions, the United States may gain neither security vis-à-vis the rogues nor continuation of nuclear deemphasis with the Russians—all while gaining a major new nuclear adversary.

In contrast, the United States should prefer to see a China that continues to deploy low numbers of weapons, a China that refrains from equipping its strategic systems with multiple, independently targetable reentry vehicles (MIRVs), and a China whose strategic modernization does not prevent further progress in reducing Russia's arsenal.

Can the United States Arrive at a Desirable Outcome?

Washington is more likely to get what it wants if it moves toward engaging Beijing in a national interest–based dialogue focused on strategic issues. Accordingly, a broader consensus is necessary about how to proceed with both Russia and China in the strategic offense/defense realm. Indeed, a window of opportunity exists for fitting China into the United States's picture of the nuclear future. That opportunity comes with the need to deal with possible Chinese responses to BMD, with the need to think through the outlines of a viable Strategic Arms Reduction Talks (START) III agreement with the Russians, and with the need of a new U.S. administration to chart a course on U.S.-PRC relations. But that window will steadily close as these decisions are made.

Does arms control offer something here? Perhaps. But we are not fully confident that it presents a solution. While China has, over the last decade, increasingly joined the arms control treaty regime, its objectives remain ambiguous. Beijing prizes the restraint arms control imposes on others but also sees it as a tool that can be turned against Chinese interests. It may not be possible to achieve meaningful nuclear arms control with China that accommodates both U.S. and Chinese interests.

But in light of the stakes and consequences, it is imperative to test such a proposition before constructing policies based on the assumption that the United States and China cannot reach an agreement that preserves past restraint. The United States should pursue political and diplomatic measures before letting the chips fall where they may in the military realm. The strategy for engaging China on these issues should follow some simple principles: keep expectations modest; build on areas of existing agreement; cooperate to strengthen the global treaties controlling the proliferation of nuclear, biological, and chemical weapons; and deal with specific proliferation problems in Asia. At the same time, the United States could do more to keep China informed about developments in the U.S.-Russian strategic dialogue.

Progress on this agenda will not come easily, especially given the intensely politicized bilateral relationship. A host of issues and questions must be addressed in Washington as prerequisites to a more comprehensive approach:

- How will the emerging U.S.-Sino-Russian triangular nuclear relationship function and how can it be shaped in ways that serve interests in stability and security? There is increasingly a need to link, both conceptually and structurally, the trajectories of the U.S.-Russian nuclear build-down and of China's nuclear modernization. Over time, these trajectories will move closer together, and this will require exploration of the consequences of this convergence.

- Is it in fact in the interest of the United States that China have a survivable second-strike capability?

- Can the Cold War, bipolar nuclear paradigm in the U.S. bureaucracy be overcome, as well as the separate track stovepiping of nuclear weapons, missile defense, and China policies?

China's modernization choices matter too much to the United States to treat them simply as an afterthought in the process of formulating policies on offensive and defensive forces and on arms control. The United States ignores China's choices at its own peril. Beijing is likely to find ways to signal to Washington that its interests are being ignored and it is fully capable of pursuing policies inimical to U.S. interests. Given due consideration, however, policymakers in Washington and Beijing may be able to cooperate and avoid worst-case outcomes and indeed to make choices that enhance their national security, international stability more generally, and mutual aspirations to put the bilateral relationship on a more even keel.

INTRODUCTION

With rare exception, China has been seen by too many American policymakers as little more than a footnote to the history of the nuclear era. During the Cold War, China figured barely at all in U.S. thinking about how to promote nuclear security and stability in a world viewed almost exclusively in bipolar terms. In the post–Cold War era, Americans seem simply to have assumed that China will do little that might complicate efforts to deemphasize the role of nuclear weapons in international politics. Because China's arsenal is so small, goes the thinking, China simply does not count for much in the global nuclear equation. As one U.S. government official said in 1998, "the evolution of Chinese nuclear force structure is not attended to at the highest levels of the U.S. government. It remains a 'middle to low' priority in U.S. policymaking."[1] As another put it in 1999, "the dirty little secret is that until now China has never had a serious nuclear force."[2] The exceptions to this general nonchalance have been driven by events such as China's first tests of fission and then thermonuclear weapons in 1964 and 1967 and, three decades later, the revelations about Chinese espionage in the U.S. nuclear weapons complex.[3]

Yet there is an alternative proposition concerning China's nuclear relevance that must be seriously considered. China may well emerge over the next decade as the country whose nuclear policy choices matter most to the United States. Indeed, its

---

[1]Michael Nacht in Ronald Montaperto, ed., *Strategic Trends in China* (Washington, D.C.: National Defense University, 1998), p. 81.

[2]Joseph Fitchett, "Chinese Nuclear Buildup Predicted," *International Herald Tribune*, November 8, 1999, p. 1. Fitchett identifies his source only as "a National Security Council official."

[3]The House Select Committee on U.S. National Security and Military/Commercial Concerns with the People's Republic of China issued a classified report on January 3, 1999, and a declassified version on May 25. Hereinafter referred to as the "Cox Committee report." For selected excerpts and associated analyses, see the special section of *Arms Control Today* (April/May 1999), pp. 17–36.

choices will certainly prove highly significant for the nuclear planning environment that might face Washington a decade or two hence. And they may also prove decisive in the effort to sustain progress toward nuclear deemphasis.

Accordingly, it is time for a fresh look at China as a nuclear actor. A host of questions requires answers: What is China's strategic posture? What is its nuclear doctrine? What is China's arms control strategy, if any? What factors will shape the future of China's nuclear policies in the military, political, and diplomatic domains? How might China react to the movement toward ballistic missile defenses, both theater and strategic, by the United States? What are the prospects for formal negotiated nuclear restraint? What does it mean to fit China into America's picture of the nuclear future?

Our study began as the Clinton administration was extending its effort to create a "constructive strategic partnership" into the arms control domain and considering how to engage China on matters nuclear. It was given added impetus by the Cox Committee and the fundamental questions it raised about China's capabilities and intentions. Indeed, the debate the committee generated about whether China is America's next peer adversary only reinforced the sense of urgency about finding answers to these questions. A clearly considered analysis of China's force posture, national interests, and policies in the nuclear domain is necessary if the United States is to best advance its interests in the nuclear relationship with China.

Without such a view, it is difficult to gauge factors bearing on the future of China's modernization effort and the points of leverage for U.S. policymakers seeking to achieve outcomes consonant with U.S. interests. Indeed, it may be worse than that: U.S. policies could evolve in ways that stimulate behaviors from China that are neither intended nor anticipated. This is especially true in the realm of ballistic missile defense, where Chinese reactions may well undermine the very stability that Washington seeks to preserve. But the opposite proposition is also true: policies crafted in Washington with a clear analysis of China's perceived interests hold out the promise of deepening stability at the strategic level and enhancing regional security.

In an effort to elaborate some answers to these questions, the Council on Foreign Relations, the National Defense University, and the Institute for Defense Analyses teamed up to lead a study process. We formed a roundtable of approximately fifty individuals from twenty-five different institutions, both governmental and nongovernmental, who met periodically in 1998 and 1999. Members of the study group are listed in the appendix. All members participated in their private capacities; institutional affiliations are provided for identification purposes only.

The report summarizes what we learned and makes recommendations based on our analysis. It proceeds as follows:

- It begins with a discussion of China's current strategic posture and modernization program. This includes a review of the important differences between what is known and what is only conjectured about that posture and program.

- The report then considers the alternative developmental paths for China's strategic force and the factors likely to shape China's choices. This includes a discussion of the impact of ballistic missile defenses on China's interests.

- This is followed by a discussion of U.S. interests in the choices China makes and in engaging China in a way that promotes the choices that the United States prefers.

- We review China's recent emergence as a participant in the arms control process and evaluate the challenges of moving this agenda forward.

- The report then suggests a direction of strategy for the United States. It seeks to build on existing commitments to construct a more wide-ranging process.

- The obstacles to successful implementation of our proposed strategy are then reviewed. These obstacles are both conceptual and procedural.

- The report concludes with a summary of key findings and recommendations.

In elaborating our line of thinking in this public fashion, we wish to underscore three points. First, this is a preliminary assessment. We raise as many questions as we answer; and many of our answers are based on information that is at best incomplete. Second, in preparing this report we have drawn heavily on presentations made to the study group and subsequent discussion at the table—all of which were conducted on a not-for-attribution basis. Third, this is a cochairs' report, not an agreed consensus statement of the full group. Although study group members have had an opportunity to review a preliminary draft and to offer comments and amendments, they have not been asked to endorse the specific language included here and it should not be inferred that all study group members agree with all of the arguments presented here. Final responsibility for the content of this report rests with the three cochairs.

CHINA'S STRATEGIC POSTURE

What is China's strategic posture? What kind of nuclear arsenal does it possess? What are the essential similarities and differences with the U.S. strategic posture? What is the nature and genesis of its strategic modernization program? In some ways, this has proven to be the most difficult section of our report to write. The hard facts are few, and their number is exaggerated by their exhaustive cross-referencing in the existing literature. A good deal of information remains hidden from view by the Chinese government, which is by far the least transparent of the de jure nuclear weapon states.[4] The U.S. government has opted not to put into the public record whatever it might know at the classified level, given the absence of detailed unclassified but official assessments of these questions. And the Cox Committee debate hints at the extent to which consideration of these matters has become colored by inference and opinion.[5] Nonetheless it important to assess what is or can be known at the unclassified level so as to minimize the risk that partisans in this debate will make up their own facts to suit their ends.

The Nuclear Arsenal

China exploded its first nuclear device in October 1964.[6] A

---

[4]We use the term "de jure weapon states" in reference to the Nuclear Nonproliferation Treaty and the fact that it recognizes only five nuclear weapon states—the United States, the Soviet Union/Russia, Britain, France, and China. Israel, Pakistan, and India are de facto nuclear weapon states but do not have the legal rights conferred on the original five in the NPT.

[5]For a detailed critique of the Cox report, see M.M. May, ed., *The Cox Committee Report: An Assessment* (Stanford, Calif.: Center for International Security and Cooperation, Stanford University, December 1999). See also a reply by Nicholas Rostow, staff director, U.S. Senate Select Committee on Intelligence, "The 'Panofsky' Critique and the Cox Committee Report: 50 Factual Errors in the Four Essays" (undated).

[6]John Wilson Lewis and Xue Litai, *China Builds the Bomb* (Stanford, Calif.: Stanford University Press, 1988).

Table 1. Stockpiled Warheads

Russia	22,500
United States	12,070
France	450
China	400
Britain	192

Source: From the nonproliferation website of the Carnegie Endowment for International Peace, May 1999. See http://www.ceip.org/programs/npp/numbers/index.html.

relatively short period later, it exploded its first hydrogen bomb.[7] The decision to pursue nuclear capability dates to January 1955. U.S. nuclear threats to China during the Korean war and again in the crisis over the islands of Quemoy and Matsu in 1954–55 played an important role in this decision, as did the growing prominence of nuclear weapons in U.S. military strategy more generally, with adoption of the "New Look" and of massive retaliation.[8] Over the decades since China has invested modestly in its nuclear forces.[9]

The size of China's current arsenal is variously estimated to range from 400 to 450 devices.[10] Its nuclear arsenal is designed

---

[7]"Beijing's first hydrogen bomb came just 32 months later. By comparison, the step from nuclear to thermonuclear took London 66 months, Moscow 75 months, Washington 87 months, and Paris 103 months." William J. Broad, "Spies vs. Sweat: The Debate over China's Nuclear Advance," *New York Times*, September 7, 1999, p. A-1.

[8]Lewis and Xue, *China Builds the Bomb*, pp. 11–34. See also Paul H.B. Godwin, "China's Nuclear Forces: An Assessment," *Current History* (September 1999), p. 261.

[9]Jonathan D. Pollack, "China as a Nuclear Power," in William H. Overholt, ed., *Asia's Nuclear Future* (Boulder, Colo.: Westview Press, 1977), pp. 35–66; Chong-pin Lin, *China's Nuclear Weapons Strategy* (Lexington, Mass.: Lexington Books, 1988); and Holly Porteous, "China's View of Strategic Weapons," *Jane's Intelligence Review* (March 1996), pp. 134–36.

[10]For basic data on China's arsenal, see Robert S. Norris et al., *Nuclear Weapons Databook*, Volume 5 (Boulder, Colo.: Westview Press, 1994); Norris and William M. Arkin, "Global Nuclear Stockpiles, 1945–1997," *Bulletin of the Atomic Scientists* (November/December 1997), p. 67; and Rodney W. Jones et al., *Tracking Nuclear Proliferation* (Washington, D.C.: Carnegie Endowment for International Peace, 1998), pp. 49–67.

Table 2. Warhead Types

20 to 40 kiloton (kt) fission gravity bomb

20 kt missile warhead

3+ megaton (mt) thermonuclear missile warhead

4 to 5 mt missile warhead

3+ mt thermonuclear gravity bomb

200 to 300 kt warhead

Perhaps also a low-yield fusion warhead

for two types of missions. One is medium- and long-range strike, primarily ballistic missiles of various ranges, to which approximately two-thirds of its warheads are devoted.[11] The remaining one-third is allocated to the tactical mission. Reportedly, this category includes low-yield bombs for tactical bombardment, artillery shells, atomic demolition munitions, and possibly short-range missiles.[12]

In signing the Comprehensive Test Ban Treaty, China has agreed to restrictions that inhibit its ability to make substantial further improvements to this arsenal. In the thirty-three years of its test program, China conducted 45 nuclear tests, a number identical to that conducted by the British but far fewer than the 1,030 conducted by the United States.

The quantitative and qualitative parameters sketched out above are in fact estimates based on the best available information. But official information is scant. China has made no public statement about the numbers or types of weapons in

---

[11] According to the Pentagon, more than one hundred of China's warheads are deployed operationally on ballistic missiles, with the remainder in stockpile. *Proliferation: Threat and Response* (Washington, D.C.: Office of the Secretary of Defense, November 1997).

[12] "China's Nuclear Stockpile and Deployments," database provided by the Center for Nonproliferation Studies of the Monterey Institute for International Studies, available at http://www.cns.miis/edu/research/china/nstock.html.

its arsenal. It does not officially acknowledge possession of tactical weapons.[13]

The Missile Force

Missiles form the core of China's strategic force. The Second Artillery Corps was founded in the mid-1960s to carry out the nuclear mission (it is roughly analogous to the Soviet Strategic Rocket Force). Most of China's missiles have ranges suitable for roles in Asia, and most of them are tipped with conventional warheads. Of the long-range strike force, only a small fraction is capable of reaching targets in portions of the continental United States—reportedly only approximately twenty missiles in total.[14] China is understood to keep its missiles unfueled and without the warheads mated.[15] It presently has no ability to launch on warning.

The emphasis on the land-based component results in part from China's apparent lack of success in developing other long-range delivery systems. China has pursued a sea-based missile launch capability for four decades, though its current force reportedly consists of only one submarine armed with twelve medium-range ballistic missiles, which apparently has not sailed outside China's territorial waters.[16] China has also devoted some effort to developing a nuclear bomber capability,

---

[13]"Information on Chinese tactical nuclear weapons is limited and contradictory, and there is no confirmation from official sources of their existence. China's initial interest in tactical weapons may have been spurred by worsening relations with the Soviet Union in the 1960s and 1970s. Several low-yield nuclear tests in the late 1970s and a large military exercise in June 1982 simulating the use of tactical nuclear weapons suggest that they may have been developed." See "Natural Resources Defense Council, Nuclear Notebook, Chinese Nuclear Forces, 1999," *Bulletin of the Atomic Scientists* 55, no. 4 (May/June 1999). See also You Ji, "Nuclear Power in the Post–Cold War Era: The Development of China's Nuclear Strategy," *Comparative Strategy* 18, no. 3 (July–September 1999), pp. 246–248.

[14]See National Intelligence Council, "Foreign Missile Developments and the Ballistic Missile Threat to the United States through 2015," September 1999. See also Bill Gertz, "China Targets Nukes at U.S.," *Washington Times*, May 1, 1998, p. 1.

[15]Robert Walpole, national intelligence officer for strategic and nuclear programs, briefing to Carnegie Endowment for International Peace, September 17, 1998.

[16]John Wilson Lewis and Xue Litai, *China's Strategic Seapower: The Politics of Force Modernization in the Nuclear Age* (Stanford, Calif.: Stanford University Press, 1994). See also "Taiwan Confirms China Building New Nuke Sub," *Washington Times*, December 8, 1999, p. A-16.

but its bombers are few in number, aged, and highly vulnerable to air defenses. They are also incapable of reaching targets in the United States.[17]

The Modernization Program

China is engaged in a broad-based modernization of its strategic capabilities.[18] These are aimed at making various improvements to its overall posture. These include:

- Improvements to range, payload, and accuracy. These have come with progress in developing solid fuels, improved rocket motors, and various targeting technologies.[19]

- Improvements to the ability of forces to survive attack. For the silo-based force, improvements include silo hardening, camouflaging, and concealment technologies, along with scattered deployment sites. For mobile forces, these include mobility improvements, through the development of solid propellants and acquisition of mobile launchers, as well as operational adjustments allowing forces to hide more effectively and launch more rapidly and from unexpected locations.[20]

---

[17] Robert G. Sutter, *Chinese Nuclear Weapons and Arms Control Policies: Implications and Options for the United States*, CRS Report 94-422S (Washington, D.C.: Congressional Research Service, March 25, 1994).

[18] For an overview and for references for many of the points in this section, see Mark A. Stokes, *China's Strategic Modernization: Implications for the United States* (Carlisle Barracks, Pa.: Strategic Studies Institute, 1999), especially chapter 4, "Dawn of a New Age: China's Long-Range Precision Strike Capabilities," pp. 79–108. See also Tim Huxley and Susan Willet, *Arming East Asia*, Adelphi Paper No. 329 (Oxford: Oxford University Press for the International Institute for Strategic Studies, 1999), p. 74; and Hongxun Hua, "China's Strategic Missile Programs: Limited Aims, Not 'Limited Deterrence'," *Nonproliferation Review* (Winter 1998), pp. 60–68.

[19] Joseph C. Anselmo et al., "Spying Debacle for U.S., But Great Leap for China?" *Aviation Week & Space Technology*, May 31, 1999, pp. 27–32. See also Shirley A. Kan and Robert D. Shuey, *China: Ballistic and Cruise Missiles*, CRS Report for Congress, Congressional Research Service, periodic updates.

[20] Richard D. Fischer, Jr., "Foreign Arms Acquisition and PLA Modernization," in James R. Lilley and David Shambaugh, eds., *China's Military Faces the Future* (Washington, D.C.: M.E. Sharpe for the American Enterprise Institute, 1999), pp. 90, 130–131. You, "Nuclear Power in the Post-Cold War Era," pp. 249–253.

- The ability to attack space-based assets, including both satellite communications systems and missiles delivering warheads.[21] It should be noted that China has ground-based defensive capabilities, including advanced surface-to-air SA-10 missiles (100 launchers around Beijing) and SA-12 missiles with limited capabilities against theater ballistic missiles.

- The ability to penetrate ballistic missile defenses. Toward this end, China has reportedly been working on decoy warheads, maneuverable reentry vehicles, electronic and infrared jammers, other technologies and techniques to defeat air- and space-based high-powered laser systems, and depressed trajectory attacks and fractional orbital missiles. Reportedly it has also explored techniques for carrying out hard kills of enemy theater missile defenses including anti-radiation missiles.

- Improvements to command, control, and communication capabilities for conducting wartime operations. These reportedly include both modernized satellite systems and secure land-line, fiber-optic ones.[22]

- Continued development of alternative delivery techniques. According to one report, China is now building 1,000 cruise missiles and has recruited for this purpose several hundred Russian specialists.[23] China also reportedly has plans to produce four to six new submarines for the delivery of submarine-launched ballistic missiles (SLBMs) in the first two decades of the new century and to apply stealth technologies to air-breathing systems.[24]

---

[21] Fischer, "Foreign Arms Acquisition and PLA Modernization," pp. 92–94.

[22] U.S. Department of Defense, "Selected Military Capabilities of the People's Republic of China," Report to the Congress Pursuant to Section 1305 of the FY97 National Defense Authorization Act, April 1997.

[23] Bruce Dorminey, "Chinese Missiles Basic to New Strategy," *Aviation Week & Space Technology*, March 8, 1999, pp. 59–61. See also "Cruise Missiles Becoming Top Proliferation Threat," *Aviation Week & Space Technology*, February 1, 1993, pp. 26–27.

[24] Paul Godwin and John J. Schultz, "Arming the Dragon for the 21st Century: China's Defense Modernization Program," *Arms Control Today* (December 1993), p. 6.

Based on a review of the unclassified literature, it is impossible to gauge how many of these intended improvements have been or will be translated into new operational capabilities. The literature implies that the theater forces have improved more rapidly than the intercontinental ones and that the force modernization program has led to an increase in the number of deployed strike systems. The literature also makes it clear that China has encountered many challenges in translating its desire for advanced capabilities into fielded systems.[25]

But improved operational capabilities have certainly begun to reach the field. A dramatic increase in the number of deployed short- and intermediate-range missiles is clearly underway. Many of these are located near the Taiwan Strait. In early 1999, the reported number of missiles deployed there had grown to 160–200, with estimates that the number might increase to 500–650 within five years.[26] These are generally understood to be missiles tipped with conventional warheads, not nuclear ones, although some reports indicate that China's short- and intermediate-range ballistic missiles have dual capabilities.[27]

The modernization program has also brought China to the brink of the deployment of a new long-range system. (See Table 3.) The DF-31 was tested for the first time in August 1999 and deployments are expected soon. This missile has a range of about 8,000 km and "will be targeted primarily against Russia and Asia," though it will also be capable of attacking sites in the northwestern United States.[28] A naval variant of the DF-31 has been planned. A longer-range system still remains in

---

[25]John Wilson Lewis and Hua Di, "China's Ballistic Missile Programs: Technologies, Strategies, Goals," *International Security* 17, no. 2 (Fall 1992), pp. 6–7.

[26]Dorminey, "Chinese Missiles Basic to New Strategy," p. 59. See also U.S. Department of Defense, "The Security Situation in the Taiwan Strait," Report to Congress Pursuant to the FY99 Appropriations Bill, February 26, 1999; and Bill Gertz, "China Targets Taiwan with 2nd Missile Base," *Washington Times*, December 8, 1999, p. A-1.

[27]See "Natural Resources Defense Council, Nuclear Notebook, Chinese nuclear forces, 1999."

[28]The citation is drawn from National Intelligence Council, "Foreign Missile Developments and the Ballistic Missile Threat to the United States through 2015."

Table 3. China's Ballistic Missile Force

	System	IOC[a]	Fuel/Basing	Range (km)	Throw weight (kg)	Warhead type	Number deployed
Short-Range	DF-15 (CSS-6 or M-9)	1995	solid/TEL[b]	200–600	500–950	dual capable	100+
	DF-11 (CSS-X-7 or M-11)	1995	solid/TEL	185–300	500	dual-capable 350 kt	40+
Medium-Range	DF-2/2A (CSS-1)	1966	liquid/transportable	1,050–1,250	1,500	20 kt	50—all retired by 1990
	DF-3/3A (CSS-2)	1971	liquid/transportable	2,650–2,800	2,150	1–3 mt	50–120
	JL-I (CSS-N-3)	1986	liquid/SLBM	1,700	600	200–300 kt	12–24
	DF-21/21A (CSS-6)	1986	solid/TEL	1,800	600	200–300 kt	10–36+
	DF-25	1989	solid/TEL	1,700	2,000	conventional	canceled?

Intercontinental							
DF-4 (CSS-3)	1980	liquid/cave	4,750	2,200	1–3 mt	20–30
DF-5/5A (CSS-4)	1981	liquid/silo	12,000–15,000	3,000–3,260	3–5 mt, 4–5 MRV?	7–20 +
DF-31	tested 1999	solid/TEL	8,000	700	200–300 kt MRV/MIRV?	0
DF-41	in development	solid/TEL	12,000	800	MIRV?	0
JL-2	in development	solid/SLBM	8,000–10,000	700	MIRV?	0

Note: Among available sources there are numerous discrepancies. Especially noteworthy are the widely varying assessments of the numbers of systems actually deployed.

[a] Initial operational capability.

[b] Transporter erector launcher.

Sources: Shirley Kan and Robert Shuey, "China: Ballistic and Cruise Missiles" (Washington, D.C.: Congressional Research Service, periodic updates). See also Norris et al, *Nuclear Weapons Databook*; *SIPRI Yearbook, 1998*, table 104.5, "Chinese Nuclear Forces," p. 442; National Intelligence Council, "Foreign Missile Developments and the Ballistic Missile Threat to the United States through 2015," National Air Intelligence Center, "Ballistic and Cruise Missile Threat," NAIC–1031–0895–98; Federation of American Scientists, "China Nuclear Forces Guide," www.fas.org, and Gertz, "China Targets Taiwan with 2nd missile base."

development—the DF-41—and is apparently not slated for deployment until late in the decade.

The MIRV Program

As a part of its modernization program, China has also been pursuing an effort to develop the capability to deliver multiple warheads from a single ballistic missile. Apparently it has had the ability for many years to deploy multiple-reentry vehicle (MRV) warheads and has been at work on the ability to independently target these warheads (MIRVs). The nature, status, and intent of this effort are hotly debated within the U.S. analytical and policy communities.

The program evidently dates to 1970 and received a boost in 1983 following President Ronald Reagan's announcement of the Strategic Defense Initiative.[29] Missile tests undertaken in the mid-1980s may have been intended for the development of multiple-warhead missiles, including one such test for the DF-5 intercontinental missile.[30] The September 1999 National Intelligence Estimate stated that

> China has had the technical capability to develop multiple RV [reentry vehicle] payloads for 20 years. If China needed a multiple-RV (MRV) capability in the near term, Beijing could use a DF-31-type RV to develop and deploy a simple MRV or multiple independently targetable reentry vehicle (MIRV) for the CSS-4 in a few years. MIRVing a future mobile missile would be many years off.[31]

The Jeremiah Commission offered a similar assessment in April 1999, concluding that "China has had the technical capability

---

[29] Godwin, "China's Nuclear Forces," p. 262. See also James A. Lamson and Wyn Q. Bowen, " 'One Arrow, Three Stars': China's MIRV Programme," *Jane's Intelligence Review* (May and June 1997), pp. 216–218 and 266–268.

[30] Chong-pin Lin, *China's Nuclear Weapons Strategy: Tradition within Evolution* (Lexington, Mass.: Lexington Books, 1988), p. 51.

[31] National Intelligence Council, "Foreign Missile Developments and the Ballistic Missile Threat to the United States Through 2015," p. 11.

to develop a MIRV system for its large, currently deployed ICBM for many years, but has not done so."[32]

The Cox Committee offered a slightly different perspective:

the PRC has demonstrated all of the techniques that are required for developing a MIRV bus, and that the PRC could develop a MIRV dispensing platform within a short period of time after making a decision to proceed.

One report suggests that the DF-41 may carry three MIRVs.[33] Another report from Hong Kong in 1995 indicated that China's nuclear test program was then aimed at deploying a warhead with nine devices.[34]

Cessation of China's nuclear test program in 1996 in conjunction with its signature of the Comprehensive Test Ban Treaty has constrained its ability to miniaturize its warheads—the essential prerequisite for deploying many of them atop a single missile. As Secretary of State Madeleine Albright has argued, "The CTBT would make it harder for . . . China to develop the technology required to place multiple warheads atop a single small missile."[35]

It is unclear how far this program proceeded prior to this point. The testing program may have halted at a point in the development process where China will find it difficult to have high confidence in the performance of whatever miniaturized warheads might have been under development. Or it may have proceeded to the point where China can utilize alternative approaches to continue development of miniaturized warheads. Conceivably, Chinese weapons designers have acquired design information from experts in Russia or Ukraine. Alternatively

---

[32] Jeremiah Commission, *The Intelligence Community Damage Assessment on the Implications of China's Acquisition of U.S. Nuclear Weapons Information on the Development of Future Chinese Weapons,* Key Findings, April 21, 1999.

[33] Lamson and Bowen, " 'One Arrow, Three Stars'," pp. 266–69.

[34] Lien Ho Pao, "New Nuclear Weapons Said Goal of Current Tests," in Chinese and translated in Foreign Broadcast Information Service (FBIS), *Daily Report: China* (FBIS-CHI-95-218), November 13, 1995.

[35] Secretary Albright, Remarks before the Chicago Council on Foreign Relations, November 10, 1999, p. 3.

or additionally, they might have acquired the necessary information through their theft of U.S. design information. Allegedly having gained access to the legacy codes for the most advanced MIRV warhead (the W-88) in the U.S. arsenal, China may not need further testing to design a reliable device. But there is also a strong body of opinion that the W-88 information is of little use to China because the Chinese cannot test their designs and in any case they lack the materials and technologies utilized in the construction of the U.S. warhead.[36]

The Genesis of the Modernization Program

The decades-long modernization effort reflects China's long-standing concern about the survivability of its nuclear deterrent. Multiple factors bear on this concern.

One basic factor is that China's missile force is aging. According to intelligence community testimony to the U.S. Congress,

> China's strategic nuclear force is small and dated, and because of this, Beijing's top military priority is to strengthen and modernize its strategic nuclear deterrent. Numerous new missile systems are under development, along with upgrade programs for existing missiles.[37]

As one Chinese analyst reports, "many of the missiles originally deployed in the Second Artillery Corps have already entered the later years of their service lives."[38] As the missiles age, concerns about their reliability have undoubtedly grown. Accordingly, the modernization program may be driven in large measure by the generational need to replace aging weapon systems with more modern ones.

---

[36] Richard L. Garwin, "Why China Won't Build U.S. Warheads," and Wolfgang K.H. Panofsky, "Assessing the Cost vs. Benefit of U.S.-Chinese Scientific Cooperation," in *Arms Control Today* (April/May 1999), pp. 28–31; and Godwin, "China's Nuclear Forces," p. 264. See also Jeremiah Commission, *The Intelligence Community Damage Assessment.*

[37] Patrick M. Hughes, director of the Defense Intelligence Agency, Senate Armed Services Committee hearings on Current and Projected National Security Threats, February 2, 1999.

[38] Hua, "China's Strategic Missile Programs," p. 65.

As it moves to field more modern systems, China is certain also to want to make technological improvements. China is essentially skipping a generation in the development of its missile force, moving from 1950s-vintage liquid-fueled systems to advanced road-mobile systems. It is important to recall that China did not mimic the breakneck speed at which the United States and the Soviet Union developed and deployed advanced technologies for their nuclear forces. China may simply be playing a game of technological catch-up, assisted and accelerated in part by the ready access to technologies now available from Russia.

But concerns about the survivability of the force have evidently been intensified by developments in China's external environment. One is the development of conventional counterforce attack capabilities that conceivably enable other countries to conduct a first strike on China's nuclear forces. Such a first strike would eliminate China's retaliatory capabilities without risking nuclear Armageddon. China's concerns about the rising vulnerability of its forces to attack in this way evidently crystallized in the aftermath of the Persian Gulf War and intensified after the air war with Yugoslavia. Television coverage vividly demonstrated the ability of advanced conventional forces to attack all fixed targets—as well as their apparent inability to attack mobile targets. This apparently reinforced the perceived desirability of modern road-mobile capabilities.

The Persian Gulf War also reinforced Chinese perceptions of the growing salience of missile forces in regional wars fought under high-technology conditions, especially missiles tipped with conventional warheads. Nearly all of China's military forces are struggling with modest resources to exploit advancing technologies in order to compete with modern military forces. However, the missile force—especially the short-range component targeted on Taiwan—has been modernized and enhanced in the hope that it will compensate for the weaknesses of the other forces. China's objective is to be able to fight and prevail in limited wars in the region while also developing the means to dissuade or otherwise coerce those global powers that might consider intervention.[39]

China's rising concern about the survivability of its strategic force has been further accentuated by the rising salience of the United States in Chinese defense planning. With the end of the Cold War, the Soviet threat to China effectively disappeared (though modest concerns about possible border conflicts with Russia remain). The United States has replaced the Soviet Union as China's primary military concern. As Chinese analysts are quick to point out, this does not mean that Chinese policy is built on the assumptions that the two countries are enemies and that China must construct a military posture aimed at deterring all-out war with the United States. Indeed, the U.S.-Chinese relationship is often described in China as its "most important bilateral relationship," with wide-ranging political, economic, and military components. But given wide-ranging U.S. influence and military presence in East Asia, and China's own rising power, Chinese military thinking has come increasingly to focus on the United States. This shift was fueled in part by the Persian Gulf War, and the recognition that the United States has both the will and the means to project power into regional conflicts and prevail under high-technology conditions. This has led to a push to develop technology for the kind of high-technology regional wars in which China and the United States might find themselves engaged. Once again, the Kosovo war has had a consolidating effect on this perception.

This is not to say that China's strategic forces evolved in earlier times without an eye to the United States. As noted above, the strategic modernization program was apparently given a significant boost in the mid-1980s by the prospect of U.S. deployment of strategic defenses (and by an anticipated redoubling of Soviet defenses) and by deployment of the Trident II system, which dramatically improved U.S. hard-target kill capability.

---

[39] For a discussion of this perspective see Michael Pillsbury, ed., *Chinese Views of Future Warfare* (Washington, D.C.: National Defense University Press, 1997).

Chinese concerns about possible armed conflict with the United States naturally focus on East Asia. Chinese leaders appear increasingly motivated to have some viable means to deal with the military preeminence of the United States in East Asia. They perceive China to be vulnerable to coercion in a way that ought not be possible in a relationship between major powers. Accordingly, the elite in Beijing seems to have concluded that China needs more nuclear muscle to deal with the American hegemon. The Kosovo war and especially the bombing of the Chinese embassy in Belgrade have reinforced both the sense of powerlessness in Beijing and the sense of urgency about closing the military gap between the two countries.[40]

Taiwan is the focal point of these concerns. Beijing apparently believes that advanced missile capabilities offer the prospect of leverage it can use to secure its goals in Taiwan without actual invasion. As noted above, it has deployed missiles to the areas neighboring Taiwan in growing numbers. During the March 1996 confrontation over the Taiwan Strait, when China fired missiles near Taiwan and the United States dispatched two carrier battle groups to the region, there were reportedly about 30–50 missiles in China's nearby coastal regions. A decade later (in 2005), that number may grow to 650.

A few months prior to the strait crisis, an event transpired that some observers interpreted as an indication of Chinese intentions in using nuclear capabilities to shape developments vis-à-vis Taiwan. In October 1995, a Chinese military officer stated to a former U.S. government official that "in the end, you care a lot more about Los Angeles than you do about Taipei." Some recall this as an attempt at nuclear coercion—as an implicit threat against the United States in the event of a military conflict over Taiwan and as a hint of more to come when China's modernization program is further advanced. Others dismiss the remark as taken out of context and bemoan

---

[40]Willy Wo-Lap Lam, "Beijing Vows to Beat Back NATO," *South China Morning Post*, May 13, 1999, p. 1.

the seeming intent of some in America to misconstrue and exaggerate China as an enemy that it does not wish to be. The former official in question, Charles Freeman, concluded that the remark "was made in the context of deterrence and in retaliation for the United States' first use of nuclear weapons."[41] In our view, the missile modernization program is not designed first and foremost to confront the United States. But improvements to China's strategic force will increase its confidence in attempting to coerce and deter the United States.

Nuclear Doctrine

What is known about Chinese nuclear doctrine? Again, not a great deal. As one Western analyst has observed, "for about 30 years after China exploded its first nuclear weapon there was no coherent, publicly articulated nuclear doctrine."[42]

In Western vernacular, China has had a posture built on the principles of minimum deterrence. As the commander of the Second Artillery Corps recently put it,

> The purposes for which we developed our few strategic nuclear weapons were to break the nuclear monopoly, to eliminate the threat of nuclear blackmail, to reduce the possibility of a nuclear attack against China, and to gain a peaceful environment for economic construction. . . . Without a nuclear capability, China would not have been involved in great power talks.[43]

Another senior People's Liberation Army (PLA) leader has summarized China's nuclear doctrine as follows:

> China's nuclear strategy is purely defensive in nature. The decision to develop nuclear weapons was a choice China had to make in the face of real nuclear threats. A small arsenal is retained only for the purpose of self-defense. China has unilaterally committed itself to responsibilities not yet taken

---

[41] See Bill Gertz, "General Who Threatened L.A. Tours U.S. on Chinese Mission," *Washington Times*, December 18, 1996, p. 1.

[42] Alastair Iain Johnston, "Prospects for Chinese Nuclear Force Modernization: Limited Deterrence Versus Multilateral Arms Control," *The China Quarterly* (June 1996), p. 552.

[43] Yang Guoliang with Sui Yongju, as cited in Zhang Jiajun and Sun Jinhan, *Liaowang* (Outlook), no. 29 (1997), p. 7.

by other nuclear nations, including the declaration of a no-first-use policy, the commitment not to use or threaten to use nuclear weapons against non-nuclear states and in nuclear-free zones. . . . In short, China's strategy is completely defensive, focused only on deterring the possibility of nuclear blackmail being used against China by other nuclear powers.[44]

Chinese policymakers and experts put great stock in China's no-first-use policy (as reiterated in China's National Statement on Security Assurances of April 5, 1995). There is an important caveat: first use has been described as possibly necessary on its own territory in case of invasion. This caveat has its genesis in the Cold War and PRC concerns about halting a large-scale armored Soviet invasion. Today it has implications for Taiwan, with the PRC sending mixed signals about whether no-first-use applies there.[45]

China has been critical of the deployment of nuclear weapons by other countries outside their own territories (and thus of extended nuclear deterrence). China also opposes nuclear deterrence against nonnuclear weapon states and has promised not to use or threaten to use nuclear weapons against non-weapon states.[46]

The small size of China's arsenal can be traced to these doctrinal concepts. If the essential original purpose of the force was political—to prevent blackmail, to have a seat at the table—then an elaborate force structure is not likely to be seen as

---

[44]Lt. General Li Jijun, vice president of the PLA's Academy of Military Science, speaking to the U.S. Army War College in July 1997, as summarized in Li, *Traditional Military Thinking and the Defensive Strategy of China*, Letort Paper No. 1 (Carlisle Barracks, Pa.: U.S. Army War College, August 1997), p. 7.

[45]PRC Disarmament Ambassador Sha Zukang stated in August 1996 that "As far as Taiwan is concerned, it is a province of China, not a state. So the policy of no-first-use does not apply." His statement was subsequently repudiated by the Foreign Ministry. See Taiwan Central News Agency, August 5, 1996, in FBIS, *Daily Report: China* (FBIS-CHI-96-151), August 5, 1996; and "Peking Acts to Undo Nuclear Arms Remark," *Free China Journal*, August 9, 1996, p. 1.

[46]Jonathan Pollack, "The Future of China's Nuclear Weapons Policy," in John C. Hopkins and Weixing Hu, eds., *Strategic Views from the Second Tier: The Nuclear Weapons Policies of France, Britain, and China* (La Jolla, Calif.: University of California Institute on Global Conflict and Cooperation, 1994).

necessary. If it had no plans to launch nuclear wars but only to retaliate if attacked, then China needed only a secure retaliatory force, one sufficient to reach out to a few large urban centers in the attacking country, to satisfy its deterrence requirements. Thus the assumption that it does not need large numbers of strategic weapons goes hand-in-hand with a doctrine that targets cities and not opposing forces.

There is a substantial body of evidence that some of these core tenets of Chinese nuclear strategy and doctrine have been subjected to growing debate within the Chinese nuclear community.[47] Because that evidence is not fully persuasive and is in many ways only inferential, the Western debate about these matters is also heating up. A fair amount of deductive work has been done by analysts monitoring the strategic modernization program. Some interpret the modernization program as signaling an effort to move from a posture of minimum deterrence to one of limited deterrence, whereby China will acquire the essential components of a limited war-fighting capability, one reflecting a shift away from a countervalue to a counterforce nuclear strategy.[48] As Paul Godwin has argued,

> Minimum deterrence, which uses a single countervalue punitive strike on cities to deter, is seen by many Chinese strategists as passive and incompatible with what they see as a future requirement for more flexible nuclear responses. Limited deterrence incorporates nuclear warfighting, which provides China with the ability to respond to any level of nuclear attack, from tactical to strategic.[49]

Others see a differentiation and diversification of Chinese doctrine, encompassing credible minimal deterrence vis-à-vis

---

[47]Johnston, "Prospects for Chinese Nuclear Force Modernization," pp. 548–76; Yang Huan, "China's Strategic Nuclear Weapons," in Pillsbury, ed., *Chinese Views of Future Warfare*, pp. 131–35.

[48]Ibid. See also Alastair Iain Johnston, "China's New 'Old Thinking': The Concept of Limited Deterrence," *International Security* 20, no. 3 (Winter 1995/96). For a Chinese reply arguing that China is not moving toward limited deterrence, see Hongxun Hua, "China's Strategic Missile Programs: Limited Aims, Not 'Limited Deterrence'," *Nonproliferation Review* 5, no. 2 (Winter 1998), pp. 60–68.

[49]Godwin, "China's Nuclear Forces," p. 263.

the United States and Russia, a more offensive-oriented posture of limited deterrence with regard to China's theater nuclear forces in local conflict, and an offensively configured, preemptive, counterforce warfighting posture of "active defense" or "offensive defense" for the Second Artillery's conventional missile forces.[50] In the words of one analyst,

> To the current PLA commanders, minimum deterrence is an awkward nuclear strategy: it is too defensive, concerned mainly with how to hide. It is awkward also because it is not applicable to any foreseeable scenarios of nuclear or conventional war. . . . This doctrine of minimum deterrence has fatal flaws, but it is an unavoidable transitional guideline for deterring an all-out war. In essence it is a "buying time" strategy, as the Chinese military commanders believe that more time will allow the SMF [strategic missile force] to develop the necessary technology and arsenal so that the SMF will not need to hide so much any more.[51]

Whatever the precise nature of Chinese nuclear doctrine today, it may be different tomorrow. China appears to be entering a debate about the utility of nuclear weapons and their role in accomplishing the goals of Deng Xiaoping's foreign policy. As argued above, some analysts are revisiting the Maoist tenets that a few weapons are enough and that China's interests are best served by continued restraint. They are considering the impact of a rapidly evolving international nuclear context on China's nuclear strategy. The planning environment that Chinese analysts anticipate a decade or two hence is a far cry from the planning environment of the 1950s and 1960s, when the core tenets of China's nuclear posture first took shape. Accordingly, new aspects of the nuclear problem are being discussed (and more openly) and new ideas are surfacing. What impact this debate might have on the future doctrine and missions of China's nuclear forces cannot, of course, be known at this time.

---

[50] See Bates Gill and James Mulvenon, "The Chinese Strategic Rocket Forces: Transition to Credible Deterrence," draft paper, October 21, 1999.

[51] You Ji, "Nuclear Power in the Post–Cold War Era," p. 246.

The Role of Ambiguity

This summary of China's nuclear posture is peppered with a host of cautionary adjectives: "reported," "rumored," "alleged," "possible," etc. The reason is simple: China has put next to nothing on the public record about its nuclear forces, capabilities, and modernization programs and plans. China stands out as the least transparent by far of all of the nuclear weapon states.

This lack of transparency may be little more than the reflexive instinct of a country accustomed to state secrecy and especially military secrecy. But we perceive a studied ambiguity on Beijing's part. Concealment, dispersal, and deception are standard Chinese techniques.[52] For example, reports indicate that in addition to its well-identified silos China has also pursued a decade-old tunneling project (the so-called Great Wall Project) that has constructed more than 2,000 kilometers of tunnels located a kilometer or so underground in mountainous terrain for the purpose of hiding components of its force.[53] We believe that the lack of transparency is intended to sow doubt about the exact nature of China's military capabilities, with the apparent hope that some will overemphasize China's military might (and thus perhaps be deterred beyond what operational factors would imply) while others underemphasize that might (thus helping China to reap the public diplomacy benefits of a military posture based on minimal capabilities, even weakness). This view is reinforced by the fact that China has moved to be more transparent in many aspects of its military planning but conspicuously not in the nuclear domain.[54]

---

[52] Stokes, *China's Strategic Modernization: Implications for the United States*, pp. 57–58.

[53] One report from Hong Kong states that "all types of strategic and tactical missiles (including nuclear weapons) numbering at least more than 10,000" have been deployed in Great Wall Project tunnels. See Sing Tao Ji Pao, " 'Great Wall Project' Said to Deter Taiwan Independence," in Chinese and translated in FBIS, *Daily Report: China*, November 26, 1999.

[54] *White Paper: China, Arms Control and Disarmament*, issued by the State Council of the People's Republic of China, Beijing, November 1995. See also Pan Zhenqiang, ed., *International Disarmament and Arms Control* (Beijing: National Defense University Publishing House, 1996).

This approach to military secrecy may well be rooted in China's military tradition more generally. As one Chinese analyst has argued, "China does have a distinctive nuclear strategy of its own which, even while evolving, manifests certain persistent strategic principles found in Chinese traditional culture" including specifically "ambiguity," "extramilitary emphasis," "the art of waiting and yielding," "minimalism," and the use of "negative" strengths.[55]

China's Long-Term Potential

Seen in its broadest possible terms, China's nuclear posture also comprises its potential to develop a qualitatively and quantitatively different force sometime in the future. What is known about the infrastructure of China's future force?

China has more than enough fissile material for a substantial increase in its nuclear arsenal. One analyst has estimated that China has enough fissile material to double or triple its arsenal.[56] Another indicates that China has an inventory of between two and six tons of plutonium and fifteen to twenty-five tons of highly enriched uranium.[57] Still others project even larger quantities.[58] The U.S. Department of Defense has reported that "China is not currently believed to be producing fissile material for nuclear weapons but it has a stockpile of fissile material

[55] Lin, *China's Nuclear Weapons Strategy: Tradition within Evolution*, p. 32. The impact of traditional concepts on current thinking, strategy, and policy is also debated. See Alastair Iain Johnston, *Cultural Realism: Strategic Culture and Grand Strategy in Chinese History* (Princeton, N.J.: Princeton University Press, 1995).

[56] Johnston, "China's New 'Old Thinking,' " p. 36.

[57] David Albright, Frans Berkhout, and William Walker, *Plutonium and Highly Enriched Uranium 1996: World Inventories, Capabilities and Policies* (New York: Oxford University Press, 1997), pp. 77, 129.

[58] Yang Zheng, "China's Nuclear Arsenal," http://www.kimsoft.com/korea/ch-war.html. See also Markov and Hull, *The Changing Nature of Chinese Nuclear Strategy*, which argues that China's warhead production capacity in the 1980s was 110–120 weapons per year and today is 140–150 per year.

sufficient to increase or improve its weapons inventory."[59] China's nuclear weapons complex is evidently sized to be able to meet any future requirements.[60]

A similar argument can be made about its missile force. According to the U.S. Department of Defense, "China probably will have the industrial capacity, though not necessarily the intent, to produce a large number, perhaps as many as a thousand, new missiles within the next decade," principally M-9 and M-11 missiles.[61] Other reports indicate that China has the capability to produce ten to twelve ICBMs per year—and has had this capability since 1978.[62]

A key variable in estimates of the possible future size of the Chinese strategic force is the MIRV program. The deployment of MIRV systems would allow China to greatly increase the number of deliverable warheads. The Cox committee concluded that China is capable of an "aggressive deployment of upwards of 1,000 thermonuclear warheads on ICBMs by 2015."[63] Whatever China's capability, the U.S. intelligence community predicts a much smaller deployment. According to an unclassified summary of the September 1999 national intelligence estimate, "by 2015, China is likely to have tens of missiles capable of targeting the United States, including a few tens of more survivable, land- and sea-based mobile missiles with smaller nuclear warheads."[64] Thus, a key variable in the size of the Chinese nuclear force of the year 2015 is whether China has the ability

---

[59] *Proliferation: Threat and Response* (Washington, D.C.: Office of the Secretary of Defense, 1997), p. 10.

[60] Norris, *Nuclear Weapons Databook*, Vol. 5, pp. 324–56; Cox Committee Report; and Jones, *Tracking Nuclear Proliferation*, pp. 49–62.

[61] U.S. Department of Defense, "Selected Military Capabilities of the People's Republic of China," April 1997, p. 4.

[62] *Jane's Space Directory, 1993–94*, p. 221; and David R. Tanks, *Exploring U.S. Missile Defense Requirements in 2010* (Washington, D.C.: Institute for Foreign Policy Analysis, April 1997), p. 3.21. Tanks notes reports by visitors to the missile production facility that the production rate may be higher than the reported ten to twelve per year.

[63] Report text.

[64] National Intelligence Council, "Foreign Missile Developments and the Ballistic Missile Threat to the United States Through 2015," p. 5.

to MIRV only the older ICBMs (the twenty or so DF-5s) or also the new and smaller DF-31s and planned DF-41s.

Despite the intense debate, stimulated in large measure by the Cox report, on the scale and scope of China's future force, the key bottom line was articulated by then-Secretary of Defense William Perry in 1995: "[China] has the potential to increase the size and capability of its strategic nuclear arsenal significantly over the next decade."[65]

Conclusion

Given the paucity of hard and official data about China's strategic posture and the strident U.S. debate about some of its aspects, it is important to underscore what is known with some certainty. China's strategic force consists primarily of missiles, many of them conventionally armed and most not capable of flying intercontinental distances. It has a modest arsenal of nuclear weapons, with relatively few of them deployed on long-range strike systems. But China has the ability to target both the United States and U.S. forces and allies in East Asia with nuclear weapons. It is modernizing its strategic forces and new capabilities are beginning to reach the field, with more in the offing. Concerns about the survivability of its forces and about possible conflict with the United States over Taiwan are major drivers of the modernization program. The old verities about China's nuclear strategy and doctrine are increasingly called into question in the light of new technical possibilities and changes in China's international nuclear planning environment. Its strategic force of a decade or two hence may be radically different quantitatively and qualitatively from the force it deploys today.

---

[65] Secretary of Defense William Perry, *Annual Report to the President and the Congress* (Washington, D.C.: GPO, 1995), p. 83. For more on this debate, see Stephen A. Cambone, "The United States and Theatre Missile Defence in North-east Asia," *Survival* 39, no. 3 (Autumn 1997), p. 67. See also Michael J. Green, "Theater Missile Defense and Strategic Relations with the People's Republic of China," in Ralph A. Cossa, ed., *Restructuring the U.S.-Japan Alliance: Toward a More Equal Partnership* (Washington, D.C.: Center for Strategic and International Studies, 1997), pp. 111–18.

FORKS IN THE ROAD AHEAD

What will determine the nature of China's future force? In our assessment, its basic quantitative and qualitative parameters will reflect Chinese decisions on three key questions:

- Will China replace existing long-range strike capabilities with the new ones on a one-for-one basis, or will there be a dramatic rise in the number of intercontinental missiles?

- Will China retain sole reliance on single-warhead delivery systems, or will it introduce MIRV systems into the forces and if so, in what numbers?

- Will China distribute nuclear warheads over a larger percentage of the strategic missile force, or will it continue to give a dominant role to conventional warheads?

Of course, some of these decisions may already have been made but will not become evident until actual force deployments—if then. But this development program is an ongoing process, and the end-state is subject to revision prior to deployment. Moreover, the program is vulnerable to resource constraints. Even if the decision has been made to buy an expensive new capability, the program may have a difficult time competing for resources. Thus China's strategic modernization program is very much in flux. There are some important forks in the road ahead.

What factors will determine the choices Chinese leaders make?

Domestic Factors
Part of the answer is found at the domestic level. China's nuclear future and nuclear strategy are held hostage, as is everything else in China, to the fate of the transition now under way.

At a pragmatic level, the fate of China's economic modernization effort will play an important role in determining the level of resources available for the modernization effort. A period of sustained and robust economic growth could make it relatively easy for China to make the investments in a large and highly capable force. Faltering growth rates may well shrink the resource pool. Of course, Chinese military planners may conclude, just as many American planners did in the 1950s, that the nuclear force offers relatively more bang for the buck than the conventional force. Such a decision would skew the defense investment budget even further in the direction of the strategic force during times of financial hardship. Moreover, many of the most significant costs are entailed in creating the production base for fissile materials, warheads, and delivery systems. Apparently, much of this infrastructure is already in place. To be sure, there would be new costs associated with increased production and the fielding of new units. But these may well be seen as incremental additions to the sunk infrastructure costs.

The political evolution of the PRC may also have an impact on the future of China's strategic force. If reform falters, the governing elite may turn even more to the nationalist banner in the effort to sustain its legitimacy. If reform succeeds, and to the extent China relates its domestic success to good relations with the outside world and especially the United States, then the confrontational aspects of China's foreign policy seem likely to attenuate. But the possibility that a more pluralistic and middle-class China could still pursue a very nationalist foreign policy should not be ruled out.

Another factor in the domestic equation is the contention for influence on policy among the various players in Beijing, including the nascent arms-control community. Constituencies in the Foreign Ministry and some of the institutes apparently see arms control as a possible tool for managing some of the problems posed by nuclear developments in South Asia, by proliferation in other regions around China's periphery, and by strategic developments in the offense/defense domain in the U.S.-Russian relationship.[66] China has made substantial investments to develop the arms control expertise within the government and the research institutes so that it can participate more fully in international processes (and so that its representatives will be more adept at conceiving and articulating Chinese interests in those processes). In the absence of an active program of warhead testing, the status of the nuclear laboratories has become lower in China (although there are ongoing investments in the nuclear infrastructure). Within the military, both the Second Artillery and the broader sector concerned with conventional force modernization are having an impact on strategic investment patterns. Of course, others in Beijing apparently see confrontation in East Asia with the United States as highly likely and thus requiring the most robust possible strategic posture.

The impact of domestic factors on the future of China's strategic forces, then, is ambiguous. In fact, external factors will probably play a far larger role.

International Factors

China's nuclear planning environment is growing increasingly complex and challenging. As noted above, the nuclear environment of the 1950s and 1960s in which China conceived the bomb and articulated its key strategic concepts is profoundly different from the strategic environment for which new forces are being built, i.e., the first two or three decades of the 21st century. At the beginning of the nuclear era, China's nuclear program was driven by the challenge posed by the other nuclear weapon states—in practice, the Soviet Union and the United States. Russia and the United States remain countries of nuclear concern to China, as discussed in more detail below. But they are being joined by a host of new factors.

One new development is the emerging nuclear and missile dynamic in South Asia. This is in part a problem of China's own

---

[66] *White Paper: China, Arms Control and Disarmament*, November 1995. See also Pan, *International Disarmament and Arms Control*.

making, with its long-standing nuclear and missile assistance programs to Pakistan. But these have now backfired on China, in the sense that more competitive relations between India and Pakistan are certain to have a spillover effect on China's own security. India's decision to bring its bomb out of the basement was motivated in significant measure by its perceptions of an unfolding strategic competition with China. China seems unlikely to simply ignore India's potential future as a nuclear competitor as it deploys nuclear-tipped missiles with the capability to reach deep into China. At the very least, India seems likely to feature in China's deployment of its conventionally tipped missiles and the development of possible warfighting strategies emphasizing counterforce and possibly preemptive attacks. If (as appears likely) the Agni is deployed on mobile systems, pressures would increase on China to supplement its nuclear counter-city strategy with a nuclear warfighting strategy built around the counterforce mission. The prospect of Indian deployment of missile defenses is likely only to reinforce concerns about the viability of China's deterrent vis-à-vis India.[67] If India moves to build the high-end arsenal that some expect it to seek (500 or more deployed warheads), an important political question would likely come to the fore in Beijing: Can China accept the position of numerical inferiority vis-à-vis India that it has long found tenable vis-à-vis the United States and the Soviet Union/Russia?

Another factor is Japan. Japan's potential as a nuclear adversary has been of concern to China throughout the nuclear era, but it has taken on new interest after the Cold War. Over the last decade China has feared alternately that (1) the United States, in a fit of post–Cold War readjustment, would depart East Asia, leaving China to contend with a nuclear-armed Japan, and then that (2) the United States, now not departing, is drawing Japan into the encirclement of China, with the revised bilateral defense guidelines and joint development of

---

[67] Gregory Koblentz, "Theater Missile Defense and South Asia: A Volatile Mix," *Nonproliferation Review* 4, no. 3 (Spring–Summer 1997), pp. 54–62.

theater missile defenses. Some Chinese scholars see these latter developments as a prelude to preemptive nuclear attack on China by the U.S.-Japan alliance. China has tended historically to overestimate Japan's capabilities, and certainly does so when constructing for itself a picture of Japan's latent nuclear capabilities. Beijing has hinted to Tokyo that missile defense deployments in Japan could well lead China to increase the number of weapons that it targets on Japan—including nuclear weapons. Relations between China and Japan are still heavily burdened by history, the legacy of war, and Japan's occupation of Manchuria in the 1930s. A 1998 summit was widely seen as a setback, foundering on Beijing's preoccupation with the bitter past, and leaving an ongoing coolness and tension in Sino-Japanese relations.

The end of the Cold War certainly eased the nuclear threat to China's north—but it has hardly eliminated it. China's thinking here appears to be in flux. Historically, China's nuclear forces were postured with an eye toward turning back a Soviet invasion (hence the shift from no-first-use to last-resort use in the case of nuclear use on its own territory). This has given way to a new set of concerns. First and foremost is the appreciation of Russia as a technology market, including at the strategic level. But there is also rising concern about the deteriorating Russian nuclear force in the Far East, and Russia's failure to withdraw it as promised. There is rising concern about Moscow's double-talk on no-first-use; the two have signed a mutual no-first-use agreement but Russia has subsequently elaborated a first-use doctrine. There is rising concern about a possible nationalist authoritarian regime in Moscow that might use nuclear threats to try to achieve ambitions in Asia. And lastly there is quiet but rising concern about a possible civil war in Russia that brings with it the use of weapons of mass destruction or their accelerated proliferation to others on China's periphery.

The impact of offensive nuclear force reductions by Moscow on China's strategic calculations is uncertain. Continuation of the process of nuclear reductions and deemphasis could attenuate lingering concerns about the prospect of nuclear confrontation with Russia. But an alternative possibility must also be considered. Deep cuts could make it seem more feasible for China to seek parity with Russia. Especially if Russia continues its slide from its former superpower status, some in the Chinese elite are likely to press for a nuclear force superior to Russia's on the argument that its emerging status as the "other superpower" requires that it replace Russia as the globe's second nuclear power.

The incentive for China to deploy a larger offensive force would only be reinforced if Russia were also to deploy enhanced strategic defenses to protect the residual force. Such a move by Russia could only reinforce Chinese concerns about the viability of its deterrent. Some Chinese experts also expect that Russia would seek to recoup some of the expenses of such a system by making it available for export to India, presumably strengthening the arguments of those in China believing that an even larger force is necessary.

The United States in China's Nuclear Planning Environment

But far and away the most important external factor in the future trajectory of China's nuclear posture is the United States. As argued above, policymakers in Beijing are focused on the bilateral relationship between the two countries and on how Beijing can use improving nuclear capabilities to secure its interests vis-à-vis Washington. The Chinese look at the professed U.S. commitment to nuclear deemphasis with a deeply skeptical eye. They flag what they understand to be:

- a nuclear posture review and a national military strategy that secured the central place of nuclear deterrence in U.S. defense strategy after the Cold War and perhaps in perpetuity, which seems to overshadow the professed commitment to ultimate nuclear abolition;

- a reluctance to embrace no-first-use, which they interpret as a sign that the United States seriously contemplates the use of nuclear weapons to coerce and even attack others, whether nuclear-armed or not;

- an active discussion in U.S. defense planning circles of the utility of nuclear weapons for a spectrum of contingencies;

- a huge U.S. technological and scientific advantage in terms of being able to advance national nuclear prowess in a no-test environment;

- a dramatic asymmetry in the ability of the two countries to target one another with nuclear systems;

- both the will and the ability to intervene willy-nilly on the world stage to advance U.S. interests and, even more ominously, U.S. values;

- and the means to fight and win such wars rapidly by conventional means alone.

In sum, China's ruling elite appears preoccupied with its own sense of powerlessness in the face of U.S. preeminence—and the possible role of new nuclear strength in remedying this fact.

Chinese interests seem likely to intersect with trends in both the offensive and defensive capabilities of the United States. On the offensive side, continued reductions by the United States (in coordination with Russia) could lead sooner or later to Chinese willingness to participate in talks on very deep reductions. A stalling out of the bilateral U.S.-Russian reductions process at a number well below today's levels but far greater than the minimum deterrent now possessed by China would raise questions in China about how best to secure its long-term interests. If the reductions process were seen to have stopped, some Chinese policymakers would likely wish to revisit the assumption that China's numbers can remain low while the Big Two reduce. The argument that China should seek parity with Russia and the United States would likely have broader appeal than in the past. If the United States were to resume testing nuclear weapons for any reason, whether safety or modernization, China seems likely to take the opportunity to use a test program for its own purposes, including further warhead development. While the two countries agreed not to target one another with their nuclear forces in June 1998, this was largely political theater: weapons can be retargeted in a matter of minutes.

China and U.S. Ballistic Missile Defense
On the defensive side of the U.S. posture, the intersection with Chinese interests is more direct and immediate. The prospect of national missile defense deployments by the United States is deeply troubling to the Chinese. As Ambassador Sha Zukang (director of the Department of Arms Control and Disarmament in the Foreign Ministry) has argued, NMD "will only poison the atmosphere, undermine the conditions necessary for nuclear disarmament, and breed a potential danger of an arms race."[68] As one Chinese analyst has put it,

> The fact that the United States is both pursuing missile defenses and sticking to its first-use policy means that it will have both spears and shields, which will greatly aggravate the concerns of other countries about the increasing possibility of the United States using nuclear weapons. This may lead to an arms race.[69]

The problem is fairly simple from China's point of view: if the survivability of its retaliatory force is already in question as a result of trends in the counterforce attack capabilities of U.S. forces, both conventional and nuclear, then any ragged second strike China might manage to launch after attack could be neutralized by deployment of even a thin defense. From Beijing's point of view, the prospect of U.S. NMD is the prospect of living in a world in which Washington can dictate to China terms any and everywhere that Washington has an

---

[68] Quoted in Benjamin Kang Lim, "China Rejects U.S. Anti-missile Defence Plans," *Reuters*, November 24, 1999.

[69] Xia Liping, "Nuclear-Weapon-Free Zones: Lessons for Nonproliferation in Northeast Asia," *Nonproliferation Review* 6, no. 4 (Fall 1999), p. 89.

interest, whether in the service of Taiwanese independence or human rights in Tibet. Chinese experts also argue that international stability cannot long survive in a world in which any one power has the means to dictate to the rest—especially a power seeking to use military force to foster its own socioeconomic and ideological system.

In the United States, a good deal of thought has gone into how to construct a defense large enough to neutralize the ballistic missile forces of small regional powers but not so large as to cripple Russian forces. A good deal less thought has been given to where China fits into this picture. This is a key point worth underscoring. In our view, the China factor has not been adequately considered in planning ballistic missile defenses. Washington today pursues a ballistic missile defense capability large enough to deal with the threat posed by so-called rogue states now acquiring long-range missile systems but not so large as to cause Moscow to lose confidence in the viability of the Russian deterrent. Indeed, finding the right dividing line has been the essence of the bilateral U.S.-Russian discussion over amendment of the Anti-Ballistic Missile (ABM) treaty.

But China is not Russia. The number of Chinese nuclear delivery systems is far smaller than Russia's and much closer to that of the so-called rogues. Unless a balance can be struck between U.S. defensive capabilities and Chinese offensive capacity akin to that between the United States and Russia, Chinese leaders are likely to conclude that any lingering confidence in a second-strike force's ability to perform its deterrence function will finally have dissipated. This could motivate the Chinese to pursue major departures in their strategic posture in an effort to resecure their retaliatory force.

Within the U.S. ballistic missile defense community, it appears that little thought has been given to the problem of finding that balance. We have encountered four primary lines of thinking when it comes to China:

- *China is modernizing and it doesn't matter what the United States does.* But we are impressed by the possibility that

China may exploit some of the opportunities in its modernization program to create a far more substantial threat to the United States, to U.S. forces overseas, and to U.S. allies depending on the strategic environment it faces in terms of U.S. offensive and defensive capabilities.

- *China's force should be neutralized because the United States should not wish to be in a relationship of mutual assured destruction with China—or anyone else, for that matter.* But we are impressed by the depth of China's commitment to not live in a world without some capacity for strategic deterrence of the United States.

- *China will not be motivated to a major buildup by U.S. missile defenses because those defenses will be deployed in ways that do not fully negate China's counterstrike capability.* But we are impressed by how difficult this will be without some further buildup of China's long-range strike capabilities.

- *China's offensive buildup would be expected and indeed welcomed as a motivator of the political will in Washington to move from modest national missile defenses to a later stage of robust ones.* But we note conflicting views in Washington as to whether defenses against large-scale threats are technically or financially feasible.

In other words, thinking in this area has not gone as far as it should.

Without taking sides in the American debate about whether, when, or how to deploy a national missile defense, we believe that U.S. interests cannot be well served by a decision-making process that has so far focused almost exclusively on possible Russian reactions. The process has concerned itself to a lesser extent with rogue state work-arounds to NMD and barely at all with the reactions of the one major nuclear power that sees itself on a collision course with America (in East Asia generally) and that actively plans for a limited military confrontation (over Taiwan). The apparent level of strategic analysis in Washington that has been paid to China by both supporters and opponents of NMD is strikingly deficient when measured against various U.S. interests.[70] This is critical to fully analyze China's possible reactions to U.S. ballistic missile defenses and the impact of those reactions on long-term U.S. interests, both strategic and political.

But China's response to U.S. NMD is still in the process of formation. This presents a potential opportunity for U.S. diplomacy, although Chinese analysts have formed a strong view of ballistic missile defense more generally, one based on the argument that such systems are destabilizing and will precipitate a new arms race.[71] They have focused more on possible U.S. theater missile defenses in East Asia than on U.S. national missile defense.

On theater defenses, Chinese opinion ranges from a visceral and emotional rejection of any defensive measures that might erode Chinese influence to a more nuanced differentiation of the types of possible deployments in terms of their impact on Chinese interests. Chinese experts appear to be less concerned about TMD in Japan or South Korea than in Taiwan. China's primary concern about TMD cooperation between the United States and Taiwan is not so much operational as political. Operationally, the PRC has the ability to overwhelm those defenses with the deployment of an even larger number of missiles, especially if equipped with the technical aids helpful for penetrating defenses. Politically, they fear that Taipei would interpret such cooperation as a de facto restoration of the mutual defense treaty and as a further source of encouragement to move toward formal independence. On Japan's TMD interests, China may well hope that it can lean hard enough on Japan so that Tokyo withdraws from the cooperative program, thus driving a wedge in the recently enhanced U.S.-Japanese

---

[70]To every generalization there are exceptions. See, for example, Dean Wilkening, working papers on "How Much Ballistic Missile Defense Is Enough?" and "How Much Ballistic Missile Defense is Too Much?" Center for International Security and Cooperation, Stanford University, October 1998.

[71]Yan Xuetong, "Theater Missile Defense in Northeast Asian Security," *Nonproliferation Review* (Spring–Summer 1999), pp. 65–74.

defense relationship. China would probably find it easier to live with Japanese acquisition of fixed-site capabilities than Aegis cruisers that could be deployed into the area around Taiwan in case of conflict.

Some Chinese analysts also speculate about the possible use of U.S. theater missile defenses in breakout mode as an NMD capability. The prospect of U.S. deployment of both theater and national defenses only amplifies Chinese concerns about coercion at the hands of Washington.

On national missile defenses, China's concern has been sufficient to motivate a substantial increase in spending on strategic forces. Announced in October 1999, the program earmarks $9.7 billion "to boost its second strike capabilities in response to any nuclear attack."[72] It may be that with time—and some jawboning from Washington—China will come to see a nuanced differentiation of interests in the various NMD architectures under review in Washington, much as it has in the TMD area. We have sketched them out along the following lines:

- If the United States proceeds with defenses at a single site in Alaska, deploying only twenty interceptors, China might not be particularly concerned. It might conclude that its more modern systems, if equipped with penetration aids, would be able to overcome those defenses. But for the moment, this option has been taken off the table by the administration.[73]

- If the United States proceeds in the context of agreed minor amendments to the ABM treaty and deploys approximately one hundred interceptors at one national site (in Alaska), China may conclude that ensured penetration by a handful of its missiles would require a buildup of its long-range

---

[72] Fitchett, "Chinese Nuclear Buildup Predicted," p. 4. See also Benjamin Kan Lim, "China Allotting Funds to Counter Nuke Attack," *Washington Times*, October 25, 1999, p. 18.

[73] Carla Anne Robbins, "U.S., Russia Elections Vex Clinton Missile-Defense Plan," *Wall Street Journal*, November 2, 1999, p. A28.

missile force and possibly also some MIRVing along with countermeasures.

- If the United States proceeds in the context of moderate changes to the treaty and deploys two hundred land-based interceptors at two national sites while also pursuing all sea-based, air-based, and space-based systems, China may seek a more substantial capacity to overwhelm both national and theater defenses, with both conventional and nuclear missiles.

- If the United States proceeds by withdrawing from the treaty, China is likely to conclude what Russians and other critics have long argued—that the United States has no intention of stopping with a thin defense aimed at rogues and intends to erect a robust defense against all comers. This could well motivate China to pursue its highest-end options.

From Bipolarity to Tripolarity

These possible Chinese reactions to developments in the ABM treaty point to the reality that as the number of offensive forces possessed by the United States and Russia continues to decline, a U.S.-Sino-Russian strategic triangle is reemerging. However, this strategic relationship is one with very different dynamics than that which existed during the early Cold War. This burgeoning reality suggests an urgent necessity to move beyond the bipolar view of the nuclear future that is the conventional wisdom at the operational policy level as well as in much of the policy community in Washington. This is a key finding of our study and one with broad importance for thinking about the future nuclear environment and the challenges of formulating policy that protects national security and national interests while also promoting nuclear deemphasis.

The dynamics of that U.S.-Sino-Russian triangle are little understood. In particular, there is inadequate understanding of the Sino-Russian leg of that triangle—that is, of how Beijing and Moscow conceive the nuclear relationship between each other and what risks each seeks to hedge against. Moscow's debate about the virtues of START has begun to encompass concerns about how China might exploit treaty restraints on Russian strategic forces to its own advantage. As one Russian analyst has argued,

> It would not be possible for Moscow to sustain a Russo-Sino arms race as long as Russia adheres to the START II ban on MIRV-ICBMs. . . . Therefore, Russia may seek as a basic provision of the future START III, a limited re-MIRVing of its ICBMs. . . . [This] could have significant drawbacks. Modification of the ABM Treaty together with high START III ceilings and re-MIRVing might be seen as much more provocative in Beijing than a package including ABM modification with low ceilings and a ban on MIRV systems. Thus, re-MIRVing could trigger, rather than avoid, a Chinese build-up. It could be argued that for Russia, it might be more important to retain a rapid reconstitution capability than to immediately adopt a provocative high ceiling. The potential re-MIRV options could conceivably play a deterrent role against potential build-ups.[74]

As China contemplates a possible future in which the ABM treaty is null and void, it also contemplates the possibility that the START process will cease and even that Russia will withdraw from the treaties on Intermediate-range Nuclear Forces and on Conventional Forces in Europe. These actions could occur within a scenario of Russia moving to reposture itself for a security environment not framed primarily in terms of military competition with the United States. Such a collapse of the arms control regime could have a significant impact on nuclear proliferation dynamics in Central and South Asia. If in conjunction with the collapse of the Comprehensive Test Ban Treaty it were also to erode the Nuclear Nonproliferation Treaty (NPT), China might anticipate a burst of proliferation in East Asia as well, to include Japan, among others. It is not inconceivable that China could perceive a substantial unraveling

---

[74] Alexander A. Pikayev, *The Rise and Fall of START II: The Russian View*, Working Paper No. 6 of the Global Policy Program (Washington, D.C.: Carnegie Endowment for International Peace, September 1999), pp. 36–37.

of the Asian nuclear environment in reaction to developments in the U.S.-Russian relationship, a process that it would want to be able to hedge against.

The vocabulary invoked in the United States to express concepts at work in the U.S.-Russian relationship is untested in this more triangular world. Is a posture of minimum deterrence among the three viable and would it be stable? What new forms of arms racing might unfold, including not just offensive but defensive and countermeasure-based? Even if Washington, Beijing, and Moscow might somehow arrive at some common notion of offense/defense stability amongst themselves, how might China have to account in its own posture for India's nuclear forces? The fact that China sits in a very different nuclear environment from the United States may preclude achievement of a stable offense/defense force balance among the three at low numbers. And how might Russia have to account for the possible future proliferation of nuclear weapons to states along its southern periphery?

It is also possible that China and Russia might deepen their cooperation on offense/defense issues at the expense of the United States. In response to a common perception of the United States as a zealous bully, there are signs of some increased coordination between Beijing and Moscow, especially after the bombing of Beijing's embassy in Belgrade. They have certainly elaborated a common political stance in opposition to U.S. missile defenses.[75] There are important limits on this relationship, however. Chinese experts have expressed a strong desire "not to set out to sea with a sinking ship"—not to count on Russia as a strategic partner. They see Russia as incapable of delivering the essentials in terms of international stability and domestic prosperity that the United States can help to provide China. The only bright spot for China in its relationship with Russia is the flow of military technology. But access

---

[75] See joint statement issued by the foreign ministries of both countries in conjunction with the Boris Yeltsin–Jiang Zemin summit, December 10, 1999.

to Russia's most sensitive strategic technologies remains inhibited by lingering concerns in Moscow about strategic competition which led to both hot and cold intra-communist war from the 1960s to the Gorbachev era.

Dealing with the 'Rogue Superpower'

China's visceral reaction to the bombing of its embassy in Belgrade is a reminder that calculations of strategic interest and of what is necessary and desirable in the way of military strength are sometimes driven as much by beliefs and values as by raw force-on-force calculations. Indeed, the future of China's force is just as likely to be determined by the quality of its political relationship with the United States (and others) as by the more arcane logic of offensive and defensive force trade-offs. The bombing had a defining effect for Beijing. It crystallized a view of Washington that until then was only under debate, in much the same way that the Tiananmen Square bloodshed was a defining moment for America's view of China. The public rhetorical view espoused by Chinese leaders often portrays the United States as an unconstrained rogue superpower pursuing global hegemony to impose its democratic free-market ideology. Yet, as underscored by the November 1999 World Trade Organization agreement with the United States, they recognize the central importance of Sino-American ties as China's most important bilateral relationship and continue to expect positive benefits, economic and security, from it. But wariness of America's ambitions and the fear that the United States will exploit an overwhelming power differential to China's disadvantage are now constant themes in Beijing. The vision of a world in which America shields itself behind a strong defense while also retaining large offensive forces and achieves status as the preeminent nuclear power in perpetuity is simply intolerable to many Chinese. Their concern is with America's intentions as much as its capabilities. It is an open question whether such Chinese concerns would persist if Taiwan were to somehow be removed as an irritant in U.S.-PRC relations. Yet China's modernization program would continue in any case, though its contours would likely change absent a requirement to plan for a potential military solution to the Taiwan issue.

Insofar as these perceptions have already had an impact on the defense investment strategy in the next five-year defense plan, on Beijing's willingness to support Washington's policy initiatives in other regions of the world, and on the broader themes of Chinese foreign policy, it is difficult to conceive that they would not also have some impact on China's strategic modernization program. Presumably the effect would be to reinforce those in China calling for a larger and more potent force.

The likely impact of the coming electoral process on Sino-American relations must also be recognized. The debate over the Cox report signaled the fact that some in the United States believe that they can garner political advantage by taking an aggressive containment posture toward China. They appear to believe that many in America are ready to embrace China as the next great enemy. The vicissitudes of U.S.-PRC relations have often been influenced by the electoral cycle in the United States, and we should not be surprised if perturbations in the coming period are still more pronounced. This will only reinforce the sense of some of the leadership in Beijing that the United States is an unreliable power and that Washington is a place where the pursuit of enlightened national interest in the bilateral relationship is chronically overshadowed by short-term political factors. If this reinforces the image of a capricious America at a time that China is debating its nuclear strategy and force, the effect again would likely be to reinforce the push for a larger force.

Notional Force Futures
Given these various technical, political, and strategic factors and the various developmental or funding decisions about the scope, scale, and sophistication of China's strategic force in the future, we are unhappy with the prevailing U.S. debate about China's nuclear future. It is too simple to reduce China's

choices to "modernizing but staying small" and "going really big." It strikes us as reasonable for China to be thinking through the following basic options.

Option one: *Small but modern.* In this scenario, China is motivated primarily by a desire to "stay in the game" but is not motivated to make the investments to do anything more than modest modernization. China would not build more nuclear warheads or substantially increase its missile force. Long-range strike systems would be replaced on a one-for-one basis and would not be MIRVed. For the theater force, there would be continued heavy reliance on conventionally tipped missiles. Minimum deterrence would continue to guide all of China's strategic thinking. In this scenario, China hopes to enhance the survivability of its force by relying on mobility and penetration aids and countermeasures in its offensive force. And Beijing bets that technical and financial issues inhibit more robust defensive deployments by the United States and, to a lesser extent, Russia.

Option two: *Minimum deterrence restored.* In this scenario, China is motivated to compete more effectively with the deployment of defenses by the United States. It would increase the number of ICBMs and their effectiveness in penetrating defenses with the goal of ensuring that roughly twenty warheads get through whatever defense is deployed by the United States. This could bring with it a substantial increase in the number of ICBMs and of deployed warheads. For its regional needs, China would continue to rely on conventionally tipped missiles.

Option three: *Regional dominance, interim global irrelevance.* In this scenario, China is motivated primarily by the desire to stay ahead of India and other proliferators in Asia, real or potential, and moves toward more robust limited deterrence strategies at the theater level with primarily nuclear forces. At the global level, China would remain committed to minimum deterrence but would refrain from making substantial new investments in a more robust force. It would accept for the time being that its silo-based force might not have a secure retaliatory capability, and it would defer a more effective remedy to some later time.

Option four: *A force de frappe.* In this scenario, China is motivated to hedge its bets against negative developments within the triangular relationship and in the regional equation by deploying a force large and capable enough to tear off an arm of even the largest adversary. Strategy would be guided by the principle of limited deterrence but not extended nuclear warfighting. Broad enhancements to all aspects of the force would be pursued and fielded, including further progress in developing all legs of a triad, advanced penetration aids, an increase in the percentage of nuclear warheads in the overall force mix, and some MIRVing.

Option five: *A parity force.* In this scenario, China would be motivated to field a very robust force as part of a political strategy to signal its ascendance over Russia, its leading role in Asia, and its equal footing with America on the world scene. Such a decision would bring with it a substantial increase in the number of ICBMs, perhaps also viable SLBM and nuclear cruise missile forces, heavy emphasis on MIRVs, and perhaps also China's own defenses. Presumably the desire for such a force would lead also to a decision to seek parity with the United States and Russia in terms of the number of deployed strategic warheads.

In sum, the possible departures ahead for China are numerous. Ten to fifteen years from now, China could well have a force not substantially different from the one it has today. But it could also construct a force with very different theater and strategic roles. We know of no reason to think that the outcome is preordained. Indeed, developments in China's force posture seem at least as volatile as are parallel developments in the nuclear reductions process between the United States and Russia and in the global nonproliferation regime.

In our judgment, in the time frame considered here, options one and five are unlikely. Merely 'staying in the game' is inconsistent with China's sense of its changing place in the world and the more complex nuclear environment that it is likely to perceive around it. Going for a parity-type force is too significant a departure—absent some catalytic event—from China's interests as we understand them, including avoidance of an arms race with the United States and preservation of a stable and cooperative international environment.

For the moment at least, China's likely choices then fall in the middle three. China's ongoing research and development of longer-range strategic forces and of enhanced offensive operational capabilities and defensive countermeasures suggest that China is moving in the direction of option two. A key indicator of the future of China's nuclear posture vis-à-vis the United States (and Russia) will be in the number of new long-range systems built and deployed over the coming decade, as well as whether they are equipped with single or multiple warheads. The probability that China will pursue this option will be influenced significantly by the nature of the emerging U.S. military posture and the U.S.-Russian offense/defense relationship.

The large-scale deployment of missiles capable of targeting its regional neighbors suggests that China is moving in the direction of option three, although the nuclear component in that force appears to remain small. The current buildup has much to do with the primacy of Taiwan among the PRC's security concerns and with the relative ease of turning out large numbers of missiles in contrast to the challenge of fielding viable conventional power projection forces. A key indicator of the future of China's future regional posture will be in whatever operational responses it may make to missile and nuclear developments in India.

Movement toward option four can also be inferred from ongoing investments and research, development, and deployment programs. The foundation for broad operational enhancements for both theater and strategic forces is well in place. A key indicator of the possible emergence of a force de frappe will be the extent to which new doctrines beyond minimum deterrence are formally embraced by the military planners and operators.

In sum, the acceptability of a decision to "stay smaller" rather than "go larger" is likely to be shaped by multiple factors, both domestic and international. In the short term at least, domestic factors and the Taiwan conflict seem likely to play a dominant role. But ultimately China's strategic posture will be shaped by its understanding of what is necessary to secure its interests on the world stage and, more specifically, to balance in Asia the power of what China sees as "the other major power," the United States.

U.S. INTERESTS

How might Chinese choices affect U.S. interests? How should the United States think about its interests in China's decision-making process?

China's highest-end options would of course have the most significant impact on U.S. interests. If China builds to parity with the United States and Russia, Washington will have lost some of the advantages that it might have been seeking in the deployment of missile defenses. If China has the will to overwhelm those defenses, it is likely also to find the means. In deploying defenses, Washington might then have helped to generate a robust new set of nuclear capabilities targeted on the United States. This will also complicate Russia's choices about further offensive reductions, as it retains capabilities—or creates new ones—to cope with dramatic improvements in China's offensive forces. This would frustrate Washington's hope of securing deep nuclear reductions in a future START agreement. If all this comes to pass, it seems reasonable to expect a rising chorus in Washington that thin national missile defenses are not enough. A dramatic surge in China's nuclear capability would likely lead to a sharper debate in Japan about deterrence of and coercion by China, and with it a rising debate about the future of America's extended deterrent and the prospects for an indigenous Japanese force. Of course, whether officials in either Moscow or Beijing are prepared to accept a nuclear relationship based on parity with the other is an open question.

Even a force de frappe would have significant capability against the United States, given that the ICBM and SLBM systems in development would have range and payload capability for nuclear missions against all of North America. In this scenario, we should expect also that China would posture its forces so as to be able to overcome U.S. defenses and also to evolve a more robust nuclear war-fighting doctrine. In this scenario too there would likely be rising Japanese concern about the viability of the U.S. nuclear guarantee. Such a buildup would certainly fuel the fears of some in Washington of a looming confrontation with China, making further cooperation to stabilize the nuclear relationship more problematic. It would also have a substantial impact on Russian national interests, coming at a time of a sharp contraction in the Russian strategic nuclear posture: during the next decade, technological obsolescence and fiscal austerity may drive Russia's strategic weapons force down to one thousand or less.

If China's force stays relatively small, the immediate consequences for the United States seem likely to be few. But even if China stays small, it will have a substantial capacity for rapid nuclear breakout, given the large number of delivery systems that might be converted from conventional to nuclear roles. China is also likely to find other ways to exert influence over developments in East Asia that it might otherwise have exerted with a more robust nuclear force. For example, China would be likely to put even more pressure on U.S. allies in East Asia not to support the development or deployment of theater missile defenses. It might also counter improvements to U.S. power projection capabilities by more aggressively promoting an anti-U.S. coalition spanning rogue states, possibly including joint development of theater missile defense countermeasures. But even China's "smallest" options will bring with them an increase in China's nuclear potential to attack the United States and its forces and interests in East Asia. As argued in recent congressional testimony by the intelligence community,

> While the pace and extent of China's strategic modernization clearly indicates deterrent rather than 'first strike' intentions, the number of Chinese strategic missiles capable of hitting the United States will increase significantly during the next two decades.[76]

---

[76]Hughes testimony, February 2, 1999.

Clearly, Washington would view the emergence of a robust nuclear competitor in China as an unwelcome development and destabilizing to East Asia and beyond. The United States should prefer to see China continue to deploy low numbers of weapons and to refrain from MIRVing strategic systems. It should prefer not to see the emergence of a more substantial nuclear threat to U.S. friends and allies in East Asia. It should prefer that China's strategic modernization not prevent further progress in reducing Russia's arsenal; Russia could well conclude that deep reductions do not make sense if they motivate a sudden MIRVing of Chinese systems targeted on Russia. The United States has an interest in seeing that viable theater ballistic missile defense architectures are fielded where regional actors threaten to use such missiles for aggressive or coercive purposes—and that China does not consider defensive deployments to be acts of aggression by the United States. The United States also has an interest in not inadvertently stimulating Chinese countermeasures that could mitigate the effectiveness of U.S. missile defense systems.

Given these multiple interests in China's future strategic force, the United States also has an interest in influencing the process by which China makes its modernization choices. Toward this end, we identify some additional interests in the U.S.-PRC dialogue on matters nuclear.

The United States has an interest in better understanding how China thinks about nuclear security and global stability. China has an interest in better understanding how thinking runs in the United States. Experts in both capitals have begun to spend a fair amount of time speculating about the policies, interests, and motives of the other side, but too often without the benefit of interaction and cross-examination. This can lead to policies based on misinformation and false assumptions. More fundamentally, the two countries are in the midst of an evolution in their views of the world, their place in it, and each other. Neither seems to have a firm grasp of the contours of debate in the other. Particularly beneficial would be some clearer mutual understanding about the necessary ingredients of viable long-term strategic nuclear stability.

Washington also has an interest in signaling to Beijing that it understands and tries to take account of Chinese interests in formulating its strategic policies. The war in Kosovo has reinforced Chinese concerns that Washington treats Beijing's interests cavalierly, even contemptuously—when it even bothers to identify them. Countering those concerns is a rising priority in U.S. policy.

We are struck by the contrast between the amount of time and energy Washington has spent trying to shape thinking in Moscow about nuclear matters and the parallel effort in Beijing. The message received from past efforts by the U.S. government, seen across the board and cumulatively, is that Moscow's choices matter a great deal to Washington while Beijing's matter little. The United States should seek to shape Chinese thinking about international security, national security, strategic relations among the major powers, security in Asia, etc., and to do so in ways that promote greater cooperation between the two countries whenever their interests overlap. It should especially like China to understand the virtues of restraint in its proliferation activities and force modernization programs, on the basis of a Chinese calculation that restraint is in its own national interest. We believe there is an opportunity to influence Chinese thinking on these questions, given what we perceive to be the nascent emergence of a debate in China about arms control and national security. But we are also uncertain of how large an opportunity this may be. Although policy experts in Beijing are increasingly interested in arms control and nonproliferation as instruments of national security and international stability, policymakers there appear more interested in new arguments about the sins of omission and commission of the United States than in new thinking about nuclear stability.

The remainder of this report focuses on how to think about engaging China in a process that leads it to modernization choices that the United States would prefer. We are not concerned with the separate question of how to think through the military planning questions that would be generated for the United States in different scenarios. The United States will have to respond as it sees fit to whatever choice China makes. But in our view, U.S. interests are not well served simply by letting the chips fall where they may.

CHINA AND ARMS CONTROL

Might it be possible to involve China in an arms control process by which it forswears some of the higher-end capabilities? An answer to this question requires some context: How does China approach arms control today? What are its interests in arms control? Does it pursue an arms control strategy?

China was generally opposed to arms control during the Cold War, when it saw arms control instruments as a means to keep the weak weak and to preserve the hegemony of the strong. As it began to emerge from its prolonged isolation and with the end of the U.S.-Soviet arms race, its worldview has changed, and with it its understanding of arms control. China is now investing more substantially in the institutional and intellectual resources to participate more actively in multilateral processes.

Over the last decade it has joined the Nuclear Nonproliferation Treaty, the Chemical Weapons Convention (CWC), and the Comprehensive Test Ban Treaty. China also supports negotiation of a ban on the production of fissile material for nuclear weapons, which would limit its future supply of materials for warhead production. It has also agreed to bring its technology export practices more fully into compliance with international norms as reflected in the multilateral efforts to combat the proliferation of sensitive technologies and materials. It joined the Zangger Committee in 1997. It has taken steps to address U.S. concerns about its nonproliferation performance not just in the nuclear but also in the missile and chemical areas. Its current practices in the arms control and nonproliferation domains now much more approximate U.S. preferences than its practices of ten or even five years ago.

But concern remains in Washington about the depth of China's commitment to these undertakings. Reports continue to surface of Chinese transfers of weapons-related technologies and materials opposed by the United States. The United States also believes that China is not fully in compliance with its obligations under the Biological and Toxin Weapons Convention (BWC), to which China acceded in 1984.[77]

On nuclear arms control in particular, China has restated its willingness to join the process of nuclear reductions at some future time.[78] But just when or how is unclear. Since the 1960s Beijing has been fairly consistent in stating its support for ultimate nuclear disarmament through multilateral negotiations aimed at a ban on nuclear weapons and full implementation of Article VI of the NPT (although, as noted above, it did not join the NPT until 1992). But China has also conditioned its willingness to do so on deep cuts in the arsenals of "the nuclear superpowers."

The evolution in declaratory policy relates to this condition. In 1982, China said that it would join nuclear arms control talks only after the United States and Soviet Union halted the testing, manufacture, and deployment of nuclear weapons and also reduced their arsenals by 50 percent. In 1988, it modified the "50-percent position" to establish "drastic reductions" as a precondition for participation. In addition to these long-standing quantitative parameters, Chinese officials have begun to talk about qualitative ones, hinting that China cannot negotiate from a position of inferiority vis-à-vis other states with more sophisticated arsenals. Accordingly, some Chinese arms controllers have praised quantitative and qualitative enhancements to the Chinese nuclear arsenal as helping to create the conditions under which China would be ready to embrace a nuclear restraint regime entailing roughly comparable residual minimum deterrents among the nuclear weapon states.

---

[77]Shirley A. Kan, *China's Compliance with Its Arms Control Obligations* and *Chinese Proliferation of Weapons of Mass Destruction: Current Policy Issues*, both issue briefs prepared by the Congressional Research Service and periodically updated. See also "China and Proliferation: Encouraging Developments and Continuing Concerns," available at the website of the Center for Nonproliferation Studies of the Monterey Institute, http://www.cns.miis.edu/cns/projects/eanp/fact/posconc.htm.

[78] *White Paper: China, Arms Control and Disarmament*, November 1995. See also Pan, *International Disarmament and Arms Control*.

As recently as 1995, China held to the position that it would not join in additional formal nuclear arms restraints unless the United States and Russia adopted no-first-use, reduced their strategic arsenals far beyond START II, abandoned tactical nuclear weapons, and abandoned research and development (R&D) on ballistic missile defenses. Furthermore, it conditioned participation on deployment of U.S. nuclear weapons only in bases and facilities in the United States and not on alert status. More recently, China has stated its position that the United States and Russia should "substantially cut down their respective nuclear arsenals, thereby paving the way for the other nuclear weapon states to participate in the multilateral nuclear disarmament process."[79]

In the current climate, however, we have a sense of pessimism about the prospects for Chinese participation in nuclear arms control beyond the CTBT. This is reinforced by an additional set of concerns. Discussion in China of when and how to join the reductions process is now tempered by a new theme in Chinese discourse, one that emphasizes perceived unwelcome developments in the global offense/defense equation and their impact on a hegemonic America. The Chinese interpret U.S. NMD as a sign of the high salience attached by Washington to nuclear weapons, rather than the opposite. This perception is reinforced by the fact that the United States reserves the right to nuclear first use even at a time of conventional preponderance and the movement toward defense dominance. These factors breed Chinese cynicism about Washington's commitment to continued nuclear deemphasis and are viewed as a signal that the United States is revaluing nuclear weapons.

We were left wondering how deeply China remains committed to the CTBT. To be sure, Chinese policymakers have promised to ratify the treaty despite the U.S. Senate's rejection of it; after all, the propaganda value will be great. Unless the United States resumes testing, however, China is more likely to wait and see if the entire structure of nonproliferation begins

---

[79] Jiang Zemin, remarks to the Conference on Disarmament, March 26, 1999.

to unravel before withdrawing its CTBT commitment. Beijing's perceptions of its nuclear future might have changed significantly since its signature of the CTBT in 1996. What it once perceived as a narrowing power gap between itself and the United States is now seen as again widening, as America prospers while China's economic boom has given way to troubled times. Its loud public campaign against Japan's revisions to its defense guidelines agreement with the United States only served to reinforce the alliance rather than drive a wedge into it. Russia is looking more and more to Beijing like the sick man of Asia—and is publicly revaluing the role of nuclear weapons in its security policy. A nuclear adversary has abruptly emerged on China's southern flank, one apparently moving to deploy a war-fighting force. The NPT looked set for an indefinite continued run, whereas today nuclear proliferation continues unabated in regions of strategic interest to China.

On the ABM treaty, China supports continued U.S. adherence and opposes amendment. Americans should recognize that Russian experts have had the Chinese ear on U.S. missile defenses for a long time. Chinese analysts have heard from Russians in considerable detail the common Russian perception that once the United States starts to build ballistic missile defense it will not stop; that once one system or architecture gets to the field, follow-ons won't be far behind, and that the first step to defenses is the first step on the path to a time when America will have achieved nuclear supremacy over all others. Hence their strong political commitment to see U.S. and Russian adherence to the ABM treaty.

We were also cognizant of the point made earlier that Washington brings nothing to the table of its own in a nuclear arms control dialogue with Beijing. The United States has offered neither offensive reductions nor defensive restraint to probe and test China's intentions, nor even hinted at any relationship between China's nuclear modernization and the U.S.-Russian build-down. Why, in Beijing's view, should China embrace further restraint when it has already exercised restraint for so long?

Does this rule out any prospect of nuclear arms control with China beyond the CTBT? China's arms control history includes a number of instances in which strict conditions have been abandoned once they elicited some concession in the negotiating process. Thus previously stated conditions may not actually inhibit China from joining nuclear arms control talks if the incentives for mutually beneficial restraint were offered.

As a study group, we spent a fair amount of time trying to understand China's arms control perspectives. We concluded that it is far easier to conceive the various (and sometimes competing) interests guiding China's arms control policies than it is to agree about whether China has an arms control strategy—and if so, what it is.

As we understand them, China's arms control interests include the following:

- *Validating China's normative great power status:* Participation in the global treaty regimes is a means for China to help capture the moral high ground in international politics and to reflect its prestige as a rising power. Some influential Chinese care deeply about China's international reputation and want it to be seen as a responsible power. Some are also motivated by a desired not to "lose face" by being isolated from other members of the U.N. Security Council on high-profile issues, such as the CTBT.

- *Reinforcing Sino–U.S. relations:* China's leaders also see the United States as the most important country in the world and articulate a direct connection between positive bilateral relations and China's overarching goal of constructing a peaceful international security environment to facilitate its strategic priority of economic modernization. They also understand the importance that the United States attaches to arms control in its global security strategies today, and thus conceive an interest in identifying and pursuing common arms control interests where they exist.

- *Limiting the spread of weapons of mass destruction and their delivery systems around the periphery of China and containing unwelcome escalation of the Indo-Pakistani competition.* After having played a negative role in aiding Pakistan and North Korea to develop missile and warhead programs, China has seen its policies reap negative consequences. A nuclear missile race in South Asia sets back Chinese strategic interests. And North Korean missile proliferation has done grave damage to Chinese interests in Northeast Asia, not least by catalyzing a new Japanese assertiveness on security issues. China may now view arms control as a useful tool for damage limitation in Northeast, Central, and South Asia, particularly if arms control offers an opportunity to inhibit moves beyond minimum deterrent forces in the latter subregion.

- *Inhibiting military developments among the other major powers contrary to China's national security interests.* China has an interest in further nuclear transparency in Russia (and in India and perhaps elsewhere) and thus may be more amenable to transparency if it can bring itself to pay the price. It also has an interest in averting certain developments in the offense/defense relationship between the United States and Russia, an interest that is easier to advance before the trajectory of U.S.-Russian strategic relations is locked in place. More generally, arms control is seen by some in Beijing as a tool for restraining the ability of the others to attack China. But there is also an appreciation of arms control's potential negative impact on China's own ability to develop the necessary military posture to counter the threat posed by others.

- *Limiting proliferation in other regions of special interest to China.* To a lesser extent, China also has a perceived interest in stability in the Middle East, in light of its growing dependence on energy resources there. Thus, it also has an interest in inhibiting destabilizing military competitions in WMD and long-range delivery systems.

But do these various interests coalesce into an overall arms control strategy for China? Our group debated four possible strategies.

One is that China now pursues arms control for the same general purposes as the West pursued arms control over the last few decades: as part of an integrated set of foreign and defense policies aimed at enhancing national security and international stability. In our view, China's interests in arms control and nonproliferation have not yet translated into such a strategy that is broadly embraced in the PRC policy apparatus.

A second possible strategy derives from the prominence of proliferation issues in the U.S.-PRC bilateral relationship. If arms control is seen in Beijing to be of more importance to the United States than China, then Beijing can exploit Washington's interests to its own advantage by linking arms control cooperation to other items on the bilateral agenda. China's most egregious proliferation behaviors have typically followed in the wake of U.S. actions that Beijing has felt it necessary to protest or counter—especially regarding Taiwan. The most recent example is the theater missile defense issue. In a meeting in Monterey, California, shortly before the embassy bombing, Ambassador Sha Zukang indicated that China was moving toward suspension of the bilateral dialogue on arms control and nonproliferation in order to signal its deep anger about proposed U.S. TMD cooperation with allies in Asia.[80] Thus a second version of China's arms control strategy is to pursue arms control only to the extent it can be exploited to its larger interests in the bilateral relationship.

A third possible strategy derives from China's effort to cope with the preeminent position of the United States in world affairs. China conceives a world order based on U.S. hegemony as nonviable because it is unjust, and resists arms control measures that it understands to be little more than unwelcome

---

[80]"Missiles, Theatre Missile Defense, and Regional Stability," Second U.S.-China Conference on Arms Control, Disarmament and Nonproliferation, Center for Nonproliferation Studies, Monterey Institute of International Studies, Monterey, California, April 27–29, 1999. See http://cns.miis.edu/cns/projects/eanp/conf/uschina2/index.htm.

props for the American "unipolar moment." But China also articulates the normative content of arms control, promotes the multilateralism embodied in global treaty regimes, and values the restraint that arms control seeks to codify among states capable of making mass destruction weapons. Thus, another version of China's arms control strategy may be to pursue arms control to the extent that it focuses international relations efforts on achieving a just and stable peace based on shared responsibility and a common commitment to agreed principles.

A fourth strategy is more base: to say one thing but do another. This strategy is inferred from continuing concerns about China's compliance with its arms control obligations and nonproliferation commitments. On the arms control component, there are two primary misgivings. One relates to the Biological and Toxin Weapons Convention: the U.S. Arms Control and Disarmament Agency's annual compliance report regularly identifies China as not in compliance with its related treaty obligations. The other relates to the Nuclear Nonproliferation Treaty, the apparent drift of China's strategic force modernization, and the fact that it alone among the NPT-defined nuclear weapon states appears to be embarked on a buildup. On the nonproliferation component, both the debate and the facts are a good deal murkier. There are undoubtedly instances in which China has transferred materials or technologies despite promises to the contrary. After all, it has provided direct assistance to Pakistan's nuclear weapons program and engaged in nuclear trade to unsafeguarded facilities in Pakistan as well as Iran. But there are also transfers that the United States has opposed and which China has forsworn. Charges and countercharges have been exchanged between Washington and Beijing in a way that has not fully resolved the issue. It is clear that China's performance, as measured by its own promises and Washington's expectations, has improved. What is not clear is how much of the lingering concern about China's proliferation activities is based on fact or misunderstanding. Thus there is yet a third possibility in the debate about China's arms control strategy: that China pursues arms control only as a matter of public rhetoric but not in a way that makes any actual impact on its military capabilities.

So, which of these strategies actually informs Chinese policy? Alas, the answer appears to be all—or none. Within the body of available evidence are plenty of arms control and nonproliferation behaviors consistent with one or more of these strategies. Beijing certainly interrupts the bilateral dialogue to tweak Washington, but it has not so far significantly abrogated treaty undertakings toward that end. Beijing certainly conceives a world order role for arms control, but has grown increasingly adept at linking arms control to its specific national security interests. Beijing's imperfect compliance raises important political concerns but does not appear broad-based. If China has a single arms control strategy, it is not pursuing it in a particularly coherent fashion.

That incoherence can be explained in part by the fact that the multiple arms control interests identified above are articulated by different people sitting in different places. In Beijing as in Washington, policy is the result of an interagency process that often encompasses sharply competing notions of what policies best serve the national interest. Consensus on the role of arms control in China's overall national strategy appears to be poorly developed at this time.

In sum, China has come partway into the global arms control regime and process. As a community, we continue to debate why this is so and the depth of China's commitment. The restraints on its nuclear forces are as yet very modest. To us, this suggests an opportunity to deepen China's involvement in arms control. The United States should begin to systematically and rigorously test China's commitment to negotiated restraint and to explore whether further restraint is possible—and under what conditions.

TOWARD A STRATEGY

How should the United States go about testing China's commitment to expanded arms control and influencing its thinking about its strategic force modernization choices? We can think of one important "don't" before we get to the list of "dos": Don't press now for formal nuclear arms control negotiations of any kind beyond those already proposed (principally the ban on the production of fissile material for nuclear weapons). China is unlikely to welcome any formal U.S. arms control initiative at this time. It probably perceives the drift toward TMD and NMD as inevitable. Beijing recognizes that Washington's decisions on the status of its offensive forces will be driven almost entirely by developments in the U.S.-Russian relationship. But it also sees START on prolonged hold. It is probably also thinking through the consequences of a possible collapse of the CTBT and NPT regimes. In any case, China appears highly unlikely to accept any restraint on its missile forces, which are the central strength of the PLA at this time and the only means available to China absent a significant power projection capability to try to coerce, compel, or deter those whose actions touch on Chinese interests.

Moreover, it is impossible to negotiate with anyone when you don't know what you're after or what you're willing to trade to secure the desired outcome. For the arms control process with China ever to result in new formalized restraints on the scale or scope of its offensive nuclear forces, the United States would have to think through answers to the following basic questions of its own:

- What is the desired mix of offensive and defense capabilities in the U.S. posture?

- What is necessary and possible in the bilateral reductions process with Russia under START?

- What modes of stability are practical and viable in the trilateral U.S.-Sino-Russian nuclear relationship?

- What are the post–Cold War missions for which nuclear forces are relevant?

We detect a view widely held in Washington that discussion with Beijing on matters nuclear would help clarify some of these questions. We detect in Beijing the opposite view—that discussion cannot begin until Washington has fully answered all of them. Getting started on some middle ground seems a desirable goal.

And what about the "dos"?

1. Work to strengthen the nuclear, biological, and chemical control regimes.

The obvious point of departure in any strategy is to test existing areas of agreement. China and the United States are both members of the key elements of the global treaty regime: the Nuclear Nonproliferation Treaty, the Chemical Weapons Convention, and the Biological and Toxin Weapons Convention. Accordingly, let us press China to demonstrate its commitment to the full and effective implementation of these instruments. Too often, China comes as an afterthought to policymakers in Washington when it comes to implementation of those regimes, or it is viewed as a nuisance that must be worked around. Some in China profess to be ready to play a more active and constructive role in the international application of agreed treaty commitments. Let us find opportunities for it to do so.

As permanent members of the U.N. Security Council, the two also share a responsibility to strengthen these regimes. This is a multilateral effort that began in the early 1990s after revelations about banned weapons programs in Iraq and North Korea. To strengthen the NPT means to utilize the process of enhanced review and the upcoming review conference to promote the continued viability of the regime, as well as the adoption of improved inspection techniques for the International Atomic Energy Agency (IAEA). To strengthen the BWC means to bring to successful conclusion the effort to add a compliance protocol. To strengthen the CWC means to fully implement its terms and conditions. The multilateral processes working toward these goals could be given a significant boost if there were to be greater agreement between China and the United States on specific steps. Continued cooperation to pursue the cutoff on the production of fissile material for nuclear weapons is also important.

Implementation issues are closely linked to compliance issues, and this in itself is an issue that belongs on the U.S.-PRC agenda. For arms controllers, the last decade has seen the "loss of innocence," with the discovery that states like Iraq and North Korea have signed arms control treaties with the intent of cheating on them. Resolving these problems of compliance is primarily a responsibility of the Security Council. In at least the case of Iraq, the council has had a difficult time in finding the right answers and maintaining consensus on both means and ends. This unhappy story relates in significant measure to a falling out between the United States and China (as well as Russia and to a lesser extent France) on how to deal with this problem. Bridging the gap, if possible, would pay larger dividends for the global treaty regime. Failure to do so would signal to violators that the Security Council will not act to resolve problems of noncompliance, as its members have promised to do.

In dealing with these compliance challenges, China appears to have been torn between two impulses. One is its deep conviction that sovereignty is sacrosanct, and that its role on the Security Council is to shield others from the excessive zeal of those who would go too far in applying intrusive measures. The other is its role as a permanent member of the Security Council, where it bears special and specific responsibilities as a guarantor of arms control compliance. Can China do more to balance these competing impulses so that it can offer more consistent and effective support to the compliance agenda? Can the United States help it to work through these issues?

As noted earlier, the U.S. government also remains concerned about China's own arms control performance. With regard to the BWC, the U.S. government reports annually that China has not yet brought its biological warfare activities into accord with its treaty obligations. China has tried to argue away this charge, to no avail. If China has nothing to hide, is it willing now to take specific steps to redress this allegation?

2. Promote cooperation on regional proliferation challenges—but recognize its limits.

The two countries have also made a joint public commitment to cooperate more effectively to deal with the proliferation of weapons of mass destruction in East Asia and South Asia.

But from the U.S. perspective, China's cooperation has so far been disappointing. China tacitly supports implementation of the Agreed Framework with North Korea, but its direct involvement in the effort to reverse that country's nuclear weapons program has been weak. China has encouraged India and Pakistan to formalize their stated intent to build no more than minimal nuclear deterrents, but its continued support to Pakistan's weapons programs has fueled continuing concern. China has promised to utilize the ASEAN Regional Forum (associated with the Association of Southeast Asian Nations) to promote transparency and confidence-building measures in Asia, but many believe it joined the forum largely in order to deflect it from touching fundamental Chinese interests.

From a Chinese perspective, U.S. cooperation on South Asia has fallen short of expectations. China was instrumental in drafting the June 14, 1998, statement of the five permanent members of the U.N. Security Council condemning the nuclear tests by India and Pakistan. It remains strongly committed rhetorically to rollback of the nuclear weapons programs there. China also sees U.S. military assistance to Taiwan as a sign of America's double-talk in its professed commitment to nonproliferation.

As argued above, China is periodically tempted to engage in proliferation behaviors deemed egregious in Washington for a variety of purposes, in many instances, to seek leverage with the United States on Taiwan. A better case might be made to the Chinese about how such behavior harms its national security interests in the effective functioning of those regimes. The more Beijing can do to dispel doubts about its commitment to WMD restraint among the countries around its periphery, the more support there will be for U.S.-PRC relations broadly, as well as increased receptivity in Washington to China's interests vis-à-vis the U.S. nuclear posture.

3. Keep China informed.

The United States should give higher priority to keeping China informed about developments in the U.S.-Russian strategic dialogue. Few actions would be more meaningful in Beijing. As it is, Russian officials regularly beat Americans to China with reports on new U.S. positions. There is no reason to think that Russians would go to special trouble to put the best light on those positions. There is every reason to think that China would believe that Washington does not take its interests seriously.

To be fair, U.S. government officials at the working level have sought to arrange such briefings but have been rebuffed by their counterparts in Beijing. It is time to boot this up the chain to higher-level officials.

4. Press China for more nuclear transparency.

China should bring its reporting into alignment with the practices of the other de jure nuclear weapon states with specific information on the number and types of warheads in its arsenal and the number and general location of deployed systems.

In pressing for such transparency, the United States must answer the obvious question: What is in it for China? China must understand that it pays a price for its excessive secrecy on these matters. That price is rising suspicion throughout Asia about the role it envisions for itself as it grows more prosperous. The price it pays in Washington is rising paranoia about the next peer adversary. The price it pays in the nuclear nonproliferation regime is that the proliferators count on China to help protect their interests in time of confrontation.

China might prefer to deal with these issues in a multilateral rather than a bilateral context, especially if it believes that the other states with relatively small nuclear arsenals might share some of its interests. Perhaps a standardization of transparency in the nuclear postures of the nuclear weapon states would be a worthy topic of discussion among the permanent members of the U.N. Security Council.[81]

5. Exploit China's antipathy to ballistic missile defense to begin a broader official intergovernmental discussion of the requirements of international stability in the coming decades.

Some in Washington have sought an arms control dialogue with Beijing, one that would focus primarily on force postures and only secondarily on the context in which force postures are decided. We recommend the reverse strategy. Seek a broader dialogue with Beijing on international security, one that comes later rather than sooner to questions of how arms control and other forms of negotiated restraint may be helpful to achievement of desired goals.

This is a dialogue that Americans will assume ought to be restricted to Asian security, but we believe again that the instinct is wrong. Washington has an interest in exchanging views with Beijing on developments in other regions where both have interests at stake (e.g., the Middle East) and wherever their joint membership of the U.N. Security Council gives them occasion to seek common cause. Any dialogue on security challenges of regions where instability and conflict are prevalent sooner or later will bring to the fore questions about how to deal with the challenges posed by the nuclear component—and by other weapons of mass destruction and their delivery systems.

---

[81]Rebecca Johnson, "Engaging the Five Nuclear Powers in Disarmament Talks," prepared for the Second U.N. Conference on Disarmament Issues, Nagasaki, November 24–27, 1998.

Among Chinese experts today is an evident unfamiliarity with some of the operational essentials: the distinctions between theater and national defenses, the specific obligations entailed in the ABM treaty, the promises made in Helsinki, and global missile proliferation patterns. But the subject ought not to be limited to defenses. Beijing and Washington ought to be talking about their strategic force postures, about the U.S.-Russian strategic relationship, about the requirements of strategic stability at lower numbers of deployed nuclear warheads.

Today there is a moment of opportunity for such a dialogue. The NMD issue has risen to a high level of interest in Beijing. The United States will not make a decision on whether or how to deploy a national missile defense before summer 2000 at the earliest. Decisions on theater missile defense are also not likely in the near term. Moreover, the bilateral U.S.-Russian nuclear reductions process has probably paused until the arrival of new governments in Washington and Moscow. Accordingly, this would be an ideal time for Washington to gain an improved understanding of Beijing's views of the kind of nuclear environment in which the interests of all of the major interested states are safeguarded. China too should see an opportunity here: to influence thinking in Washington and Moscow before the two set off on a new trajectory of nuclear diplomacy in 2001.

On defenses, it is clear that China knows what it does *not* want: deployment of ballistic missile defenses by the United States and/or its allies. Yet it does not appear to know what it wants in the form of stable military relations in the region, other than the upper hand that it appears to seek with the qualitative and quantitative improvements to its strategic force. This perception is fueled by China's ongoing modernization of its own ballistic missiles—a program that has generated considerable concern, even fear, among countries in Northeast Asia, Southeast Asia, and South Asia. The situation in East Asia today in some ways mirrors the situation in Europe in the early 1980s, as the Soviets engaged in a massive buildup of intermediate-range missile systems. Is there an arms control opportunity in East Asia, analogous to the Treaty on Intermediate-range Nuclear Forces in Europe, that could remove the missile problem? Or must the United States and its allies rely on a military response?

Lastly, we think government experts in Washington and Beijing will not have covered the landscape if they explore only offense and defense issues in the bilateral relationship. As argued above, a tripolar U.S.-Sino-Russian relationship is emerging. Few analysts—whether in Beijing, Moscow, or Washington—think about the world in tripolar terms. Fewer yet understand the complex interaction of offense and defense among the three at the strategic level. China has an interest in shaping this tripolar interrelationship so that it does not have to invest in significant modernization of its strategic forces. From an American perspective, it is probably not helpful that China continues to articulate positions on future nuclear reductions that appear to be based on policies that long predate the current strategic era. Is there new thinking in China about the trilateral reductions process?

If dialogue on these subjects is to have an impact on policy, it must be conducted at the official level. Formal but wide-ranging exchanges among policy planning staffs could contribute significantly to the goals sketched out above. We believe that this will require a new framework at the most senior levels, as argued in more detail below.

This discussion of venues raises a question about what the so-called track two or track one-and-a-half nongovernmental or quasi-governmental processes can contribute. Such processes have a role to play. They are useful for exploring policy options and strategic perspectives on big problems without the obstacles posed by formal conditions. They are also very active in the Asia-Pacific region. But these processes also have their limits. Their influence on policymakers in Beijing is not well demonstrated. They can create the appearance of dialogue without its substance. In our view, on this agenda, such processes can play a particularly useful role in advancing U.S.-Chinese under-standing of the requirements of strategic stability, features of alternative nuclear futures, and political-military dynamics in the trilateral relationship. But this will require improved coordi-nation among the nongovernmental organizations and between the NGOs and the U.S. interagency process.

OBSTACLES

Practically speaking, what are the prospects for the success of the policy agenda elaborated above? In our view, we have sketched out what is essentially a prelude to a strategy—a way to test the waters, to advance thinking and dialogue, to probe and prod. An integrated political-military response to China's strategic modernization should follow this effort.

Our hope that this agenda can succeed is tempered by the experience of the Clinton administration, which, after all, has tried to open a door to strategic dialogue with Beijing on matters nuclear. But this dialogue has not gotten much beyond square one, for many of the reasons outlined above. The ballistic missile defense issue has become a stalking horse for anxieties and ambitions in both countries. For these and other reasons, there has not been much of a dialogue on missile defense between the two countries; rather, they have engaged in "dueling talking points."

Part of the problem may well be that U.S. arms controllers too often sound like evangelists, trying to win converts to their cause. The Chinese rightly observe that what works for one country—particularly one with so many strengths—may not work for another—particularly one with so many weaknesses. The strong can afford to trade away excess strength, goes the argument, while the weak must nurture what assets they've got. The goal should be to talk with China in national interest terms. Americans need to get better at talking with the Chinese about how future negotiated restraints might bring further improvements to China's security environment and help it to avoid costs and risks.

But the obstacles to success are more numerous and extensive. Some are clearly on the Chinese side. China's history and habits of dealing with matters of core national security are highly insular and closed. It may be that to challenge these habits is to challenge the mode of governance of an authoritarian state. Given its reactions to the Falun Gong group and political dissidents, the governing elite also appears to see itself as highly vulnerable and thus is likely to be risk averse. That government also voices "concession fatigue" in dealing with Washington. Moreover, Chinese negotiators appear to believe that trust is the essential prerequisite to dialogue, in contrast to Americans, who believe that dialogue builds trust.

To overcome some of these obstacles in China to the agenda sketched out in the previous section, we believe that the administration needs to make the strongest possible case of what is in it for China. We believe it should press especially hard on the following Chinese interests.

First, China has an interest in influencing decisions that Washington and Moscow are getting ready to make soon. Decision-makers in both capitals appear poised to make a series of decisions on the offense/defense relationship between them that are going to have an impact on China's interests. China's interests would be better served by shaping those decisions ahead of time in ways that meet China's security requirements, than by being stuck to protest those decisions or cope with their consequences, perhaps in expensive and politically taxing ways. Whether the current administration in Washington can cut a definitive deal with the current administration in Moscow is an open question; it seems very likely that after presidential elections in both countries, the two will renew some sort of arms control process. Waiting to get involved analytically and politically until that time could prove harmful to China.

Second, China has an interest in avoiding arms races. There is the prospect of formal negotiated restraint by Russia and the United States that would ease the military planning burden on China. China, Russia, and the United States may be able to work together to find an offense/defense system that helps to reduce the operational requirements on Chinese forces.

But the obstacles are not only in Beijing. They are also in Washington. One is the simple fact that the United States has a lot of homework to do. We need to puzzle through how the emerging triangular U.S.-Sino-Russian nuclear relationship will function and should be shaped. It is simply intellectual terra incognita. Is a parity-based relationship in the U.S. interest? Is three-way mutually assured destruction (MAD) possible and/or desirable? Can a triangular relationship be stable? And by what measures? Can the triangle be isolated from the presence of other nuclear actors in Asia?

But there is a much harder question that needs an answer: Is it in the interest of the United States for China to have a survivable second-strike capability? For some in the U.S. debate, the answer is an obvious yes. China's sense of security requires that it not conceive itself the victim of nuclear coercion or attack, and thus Washington has an interest in finding common ground with China on the necessary ingredients of that survivable capability. For others in the debate, the answer is an obvious no: the United States should never again have to live in a world of mutual assured destruction, and thus Washington should field the mix of offense and defense and nuclear and nonnuclear forces that ensure this outcome. The absence of consensus on this question seems likely to deeply impair the ability of the United States to create a negotiating framework with China on nuclear matters that is viable in the long term.

There is another hard question that belongs on the U.S. agenda: Is there any basis for compromise with China on the issue of no-first-use? If there were such a basis, one important source of Chinese anxiety about the nuclear threat posed by the United States could be alleviated. As noted earlier, Chinese experts interpret Washington's refusal to forswear first use of nuclear weapons as a sign that the United States actively considers and plans for preemptive nuclear attack on China. Washington's current opposition to no-first-use has little or nothing to do with China, and arises instead from concern about deterring regional aggressors with weapons of mass destruction and the credibility of U.S. security assurances—of extended deterrence—particularly in the case of Japan. China would benefit from a clearer understanding of the basis of U.S. policy. The United States would benefit from engaging China in a discussion of regional conflicts against aggressors armed with weapons of mass destruction. If the result were also a revised U.S. declaratory policy, perhaps a pledge of no-first-use of WMD, the two countries might find some new basis for further cooperation in minimizing nuclear risks.

This homework will be all the harder for the simple reason that the constellations of expertise necessary to complete the assignment have not been brought together adequately. The U.S. strategic nuclear community remains heavily focused on the U.S.-Russian relationship. The ballistic missile defense community is heavily focused on the technical problems associated with a fix to the vulnerability problem. The country specialists are well versed in the political dynamic between the two countries but have little familiarity with matters nuclear or often with political-military affairs more generally. The makers of foreign policy and the makers of defense policy do not show many public signs of having coordinated their activities. It has become a post–Cold War fad in Washington to criticize "stovepiping"; but here is yet another place where we pay a price for our slow progress in generating new constellations of expertise.

There is a more general obstacle as well: Washington's difficulty in pursuing a coherent and consistent policy vis-à-vis China. Beijing perceives the bilateral relationship as regularly taken hostage by special interests in Washington that do not understand either Chinese interests or U.S. interests in a stable and cooperative relationship. Chinese experts understand that a nuclear buildup will reinforce U.S. perceptions of China as the next great enemy. Most of them appear to prefer that to perceptions of Chinese impotence and irrelevance.

KEY FINDINGS AND RECOMMENDATIONS

Force Modernization

1. *China is modernizing its strategic forces in ways that could lead to major departures in the scale, scope, purpose, and function of those forces.* Beijing aims at an across-the-board improvement of its forces and during the last two decades has invested substantially in infrastructure and technology.

2. *This modernization will continue regardless of what Washington chooses to do, but the ultimate shape of the force remains an open question.* The final determination will depend upon ongoing Chinese assessments of a wide range of political, military, technological, and strategic factors.

3. *Chinese modernization decisions are driven substantially by long-standing concerns about the survivability of its retaliatory force.* China views its new ICBM, the DF-31, as providing a survivable second-strike capacity. Chinese concerns intensified as Washington deployed long-distance, precision, conventional strike capabilities and demonstrated their effectiveness in the Gulf War and in Yugoslavia.

4. *Although China is widely reported to have deployed about twenty ballistic missiles capable of reaching the continental United States, the actual number may well be different— whether higher or lower we cannot judge.* But it is clear that Beijing will field a new generation of long-range mobile missiles that have such capability.

5. *Beijing can deploy multiple warheads atop its current long-range missiles, although it has chosen not to do so.* However, its ability to MIRV its new missiles is uncertain. Collapse of the CTBT could remove a significant obstacle in this area.

Strategy

6. *Minimum deterrence apparently remains the foundation of Beijing's intercontinental doctrine at this time.* However, there are multiple signs of an increasingly vigorous debate on nuclear strategy. Moreover, new technical possibilities and perceived changes in China's external environment may lead to a more differentiated strategy, including limited deterrence and nuclear counterforce missions.

7. *Beijing's marked lack of transparency stands in sharp contrast to the four other de jure nuclear weapons states.* It is almost certainly an integral facet of its nuclear strategy.

8. *China appears to have begun a mirror-image process of worst-case military planning in response to U.S. plans and discussion of missile defense deployments.* Concerns about the credibility of Beijing's nuclear deterrent in the event of U.S. deployment of national missile defenses are a significant element in China's nuclear planning.

Missile Defense

9. *The prospect of missile defense deployments by the United States, both in theater and at the national level, intensifies Chinese concerns about force capability and effectiveness.* The prospect also fuels Beijing's concerns about Taiwanese independence and especially about potential longer-term U.S. containment objectives.

10. *It is worth emphasizing that the Taiwan issue is central to Beijing's strategic worldview, influencing Chinese views on virtually all issues, including missile defense.* For example, Chinese concerns about U.S. deployment of theater and national ballistic missile defenses are intensified by the possibility of military confrontation over Taiwan.

11. *BMD decisions could have unintended consequences.* Possible Russian reactions to possible U.S. withdrawal from the

ABM treaty are especially disconcerting to Beijing. A major buildup by Moscow would clearly not be in Beijing's interest. On the other hand, rhetoric in Beijing and Moscow is strongly opposed to U.S. missile defense plans that have already been announced, and there are indications of growing strategic cooperation between the two. Such cooperation does not serve U.S. interests and could provoke the transfer to China of advanced Russian defense countermeasures.

12. *It is not clear what Beijing's response will be.* It might seek to restore the status quo ante by increasing the size of the force to the point at which U.S. missile defense would be overwhelmed. Or it might deploy a much larger force capable of implementing strategies beyond minimum deterrence. Whatever the decision, U.S. deployments will be used as a rationalization of China's actions.

U.S. Policy

13. *The United States has an interest in not seeing China emerge as a major nuclear competitor.* A political understanding may make this possible, whether an arms control agreement or something less formal.

14. *There has been insufficient recognition of the importance of China's modernization choices to the United States.*

15. *Policy on nuclear weapons and arms control has remained largely bipolar in nature, focusing on the U.S.-Russian relationship.* The bipolar paradigm has obscured the emerging triangular strategic offense/defense relationship among the United States, China, and Russia. This is intellectual terra incognita.

16. *There is increasingly a need to link—both conceptually and structurally—the trajectories of the U.S.-Russian nuclear build-down and of China's nuclear modernization.* Over time, the trajectories will move closer together. This requires exploration of the consequences of this convergence.

17. *Stovepiping is a serious problem in the U.S. policy process.* Policies on nuclear weapons, missile defense, and China tend to operate on three separate tracks, making it difficult to take into account and balance interests that sometimes compete or conflict.

18. *The United States and China today have a window of opportunity to address these issues.* Opportunities will narrow as Washington makes decisions on theater and national missile defenses and on a START III negotiating position vis-à-vis Russia.

19. *It may not be possible to achieve meaningful arms control with China that satisfactorily accommodates both U.S. and Chinese interests.* In light of the stakes and consequences it is imperative to fully and fairly test that proposition before arriving at such a conclusion.

Recommendations

1. *Come to terms with core issues.* Before engaging China on arms control issues, the United States needs to address such questions as: What is the role of nuclear weapons in its post–Cold War defense strategy? For what post–Cold War missions are nuclear forces relevant? What force levels are required at what state of alert? What is the desired mix of offense and defense in the U.S. posture? Whatever the process—whether high-level commission or a renewed nuclear posture review—answers to these questions must be informed by a clear view of China.

2. *Work out the appropriate tripolar paradigm for nuclear arms control.* The conceptual framework for determining the end-state of the U.S.-Russia build-down should be adjusted to fully reflect the emerging strategic triangle and the interaction of decisions in Washington, Moscow, and Beijing. Because China is the only declared nuclear weapon state that is increasing both qualitatively and quantitatively its nuclear forces, its modernization trajectory will, over

time, move into closer proximity with the U.S.-Russian build-down trajectory.

3. *Recognize that strategic issues are an important component in U.S.-PRC relations.* The United States and China need to exchange assessments of factors favoring and undercutting international stability in the coming decades and allow arms control implications to follow logically from this process. Beijing's strong reaction to ballistic missile defense offers an excellent opportunity to begin such high-level discussions.

4. *Move aggressively to deal with the negative consequences of stovepiping by creating mechanisms for coordinating different bureaucratic perspectives and priorities.* This should be overseen by the National Security Council. The NGO community also has a role to play in generating crosscutting approaches. Its ability to contribute would be improved if there were stronger cooperation within the community as well as enhanced coordination with official efforts. This can also be extended to the Chinese arms control and foreign policy communities.

5. *Enhance cooperation with China on arms control and nonproliferation where there appear to be overlapping interests, both global and regional.* But keep expectations modest.

6. *Work with the other permanent members of the U.N. Security Council, as well as in regional venues, to persuade Beijing that increased transparency is in its national interest.*

7. *Incorporate a considered understanding of possible Chinese responses into plans for ballistic missile defenses, both theater and strategic.* Certain deployment plans may achieve U.S. objectives without generating unwelcome Chinese responses.

8. *Incorporate a considered understanding of interactions between Russian and Chinese force planning and preparations into follow-on strategic arms control proposals to Russia.* START

III provisions on MIRVs and up-loads may have to account for possible Chinese reactions.

9. *Begin to test China's intentions by exploring what restraint it is prepared to demonstrate in exchange for certain forms of U.S. restraint.* This discussion should begin at a policy planning level between governments and perhaps at a track one-and-a-half, officially sanctioned, officially deniable NGO level.

10. *In considering an arms control approach to China, we should seek to understand how such engagement and any agreements that might be reached would affect U.S. nuclear strategy and the linkage to U.S. forward-deployed forces in various scenarios.* We also need to anticipate the impact of such engagement on U.S. allies in the region, given their dependence on U.S. extended deterrence. This requires examining in greater analytical detail Chinese modernization options, the objectives they may serve, and the potential impact of each on the regional security environment.

APPENDIX

ROUNDTABLE MEMBERS

Ken Allen, Stimson Center
Richard Betts, Council on Foreign Relations
Zachary Davis, Congressional Research Service
Jason Ellis, National Defense University
Wendy Frieman, George Washington University
Banning Garrett, Center for Strategic and International Studies
Bates Gill, Brookings Institution
Bonnie Glaser, consultant
Jo Husbands, National Academy of Sciences
Frank Jenkins, Science Applications International Corp.
Shirley Kan, Congressional Research Service
Michael Krepon, Stimson Center
Robert Manning, Council on Foreign Relations
Thomas Marfiak, National War College
Mike McDevitt, Center for Naval Analyses
Eric McVadon, consultant
Lyman Miller, Johns Hopkins University, School of Advanced
    International Studies
Ronald Montaperto, National Defense University
James Mulvenon, RAND Corporation
Michael Nacht, University of California
James Przystup, National Defense University
Brad Roberts, Institute for Defense Analyses
Lawrence Scheinman, Monterey Institute of
    International Studies
David Shambaugh, George Washington University
Robert Suettinger, Brookings Institution

Editor's Note: Among the government agencies represented in the discussions as observers were the Departments of State, Defense, and Energy, as well as the intelligence community. Government officials participated in their private capacities.